REWRITE
YOUR DESTINY

REWRITE YOUR DESTINY

THE POWER WITHIN US TO CHANGE EVERYTHING

SHERIFE ABDELMESSIH

R

RINASCENTE

NEW YORK

Published in the United States in 2024
1st Printing

R
Rinascente
New York

ISBN 979-8-9879606-2-2 (paperback)
ISBN 979-8-9879606-4-6 (ebook)

Also by Sherife AbdelMessih

Super Vision: An Eye-Opening Approach to Getting Unstuck

To FDL

for saving my life…

CONTENTS

PART III: REDESIGN YOUR RELATIONSHIPS

INTRODUCTION

What is destiny? Is life a screenplay that has already been written for us? Are we just actors playing out a plot that has been set long ago? Would life have any meaning if this was our reality? Wouldn't we all just be robots, moving at a precisely calculated and predetermined pace and direction?

If we look at science for guidance, we can see that such a world does not exist. The universe is full of chaos; change is the only constant. It would not make sense that we humans, the most sophisticated species we know of in the universe, would depart from the laws of entropy and be confined by some rigid script that we must act out. Quantum physics assures us that even if it were possible to measure everything that is measurable, the unpredictability of the world would still persist.

Some of you will prefer these scientific explanations for our existence, while others believe in the existence of God and more spiritual explanations for our creation. I want to communicate with both. If there was an intelligent designer that created us, a common argument for the existence of God, would such a Deus have devised a gigantic play with trillions of characters that have no free will—no say in their lives? I can't believe that God would be so sadistic or derive any pleasure from such a boring story. There would be no meaning in that.

You cannot love someone if you do not give them their freedom and everyone that believes in God has been taught that he loves us. Consequently, God could not have created us as slaves to a predestined story that we must act out. God either created us free because he loves us or created us as slaves with no free will because he does not. The argument also falls on its head when we ask ourselves why there is so much pain in the world, whether it's murder, rape, or war. If God has already chosen our destiny for us, how could he instruct humanity to engage in all of this? The only explanation is that he has given us free will. The only answer is that it is us humans that choose to rape and murder against God's wishes.

So, if our destiny is not predetermined, how *is* it shaped? We can think of destiny as a coin with two sides. On one side, there are the events that happen to us, like how the weather turns out to be rainy on the day of our big football game. On the other side, there is how we choose to respond to these events, like how we decide to play the game in response to the weather. Do we allow the bad weather to dampen our spirits and prevent us from giving our best, or do we use it as fuel to play ferociously because we will not allow a little rain to rob us of our glory?

There are many factors in life that are completely beyond our control. Our facial features, the family and place we were born into, the people that walk into and out of our lives, and many other crucial events. Whether we call this destiny or not doesn't have much relevance because, regardless of what name we bestow upon it, it is not something we can change. There is something, however, that is much more important than this initial set of *uncontrollable factors*. It is how *we respond* to them. This is what determines our destiny and it is ultimately how we can shape it.

Millions of soldiers are sent to war, but are they all the same when they come back? Hundreds of millions of people suffer from the same disease, but does it impact their lives in the same way? There are people throughout history who have experienced crippling circumstances, yet they have managed to achieve more in life than people with more fortunate lives.

You are the master of your own destiny; the captain of your ship. You may have no control over the weather nor the direction that the wind blows, but you must learn to muster the courage to steer your ship toward your desired destination as you factor in the changes in the weather. A tennis player does not control the point at which they will receive the ball, but they control the direction in which they will send it back. There is no one location where they must receive the ball in order to win the game. Their ability to win lies not in the uncontrolled destiny of where the ball will be received but in the controlled destiny of how they decide to retrieve the ball and send it back across the net.

To rewrite our destiny, we must first develop the wisdom to recognize the events we must change and the ones we should accept; those we must work to alter in our best interests, and the ones we must change the way we feel about. There is a sagacity to recognizing that just because we want something, doesn't mean that this is the right time or place for it. There is a need to discern which of our desires should be pursued and which we should strip ourselves of.

Once you realize the power you have to rewrite your destiny, you will be able to live a much more enjoyable and impactful life. It's empowering to understand the strength that lies within all of us to change our path or the suppleness to embrace it if we decide to. I look forward to taking you on this journey. We can move mountains when it comes to rewriting our destiny, even though it might seem that some mountains in our life are unmovable.

PART I

DISCOVER THE ENEMY WITHIN

The future is ours to shape

But so is the past

We spend so much time trying to heal from the past

Because we've been told that we can't change the past

Oh, but we can…

ONE

SUBCONSCIOUS FABRICATIONS

As long as you don't make the subconscious conscious, it will direct your life and you will call it fate.

—Friedrich Nietzsche

R emember that charming person you once met whom you felt something for? But, for some reason, mysteriously, you decided not to give them a shot and see where it went... What about that idea you really wanted to pursue? But you never did because you felt, instinctively, there were good reasons why you couldn't. Does this sound familiar?

What do these experiences have in common? For you, me, and millions of other people, it's our subconscious mind that's behind this reluctance. Many times, it prevents us from pursuing something that could allow us to progress in our lives. Our subconscious mind has good intentions—it is trying to protect us—but, in many cases, it ends up handicapping us instead.

Let me tell you a story from my life that demonstrates this well. It was when I first became aware of how much mental and emotional pain people were suffering. I desperately wanted to help them and, after much reflection, I had an idea; something that could really help people to regulate their emotions and be happier. Everyone loved it. And by everyone, I mean big businessmen and industry experts as well as friends and students. The response I got was overwhelming. At the time, I didn't have the background or expertise in this field to turn the idea into reality. But I felt that this was my calling to rise to the occasion. So, I decided to go on an uphill journey of experimentation and learning. I had to get to grips with three different industries and merge my insights together into one product. I created a new company around it, built a team, and poured my life into this venture. I worked around the clock bringing it to fruition, getting very little sleep in the process. I also spent a fortune as I set up my headquarters in SoHo, New York—the design capital of the world—which also happens to be one of the most expensive places to live and work.

After two years of blood, sweat, and tears, it became clear to me that it wasn't working. After the incessant cries of those closest to me, I finally decided to pull the plug. It was the hardest decision I had ever made and still is. This created an existential crisis for me at the time. I felt lost. How could I be penalized for my goodwill and all the sacrifices I'd made? How could this fail?

In the aftermath of this devastation, I felt I had to recover the money I'd lost. The logical decision was for me to spend my time on a business opportunity that had the highest certainty of making money. I couldn't afford to take big risks at that moment. Coincidentally, around that time, one of the subsidiaries of my renewable energy company started having trouble. Let's call this subsidiary Jade. The company was in the Caribbean, where electricity prices are some of the highest in the world, making the company very lucrative. I had founded that company when

I was in my early twenties. It only took a few years of smart decisions, the right partnerships, strategic thinking, and surgical execution to turn the company into the leader in the region. But now it was in trouble, with revenue falling.

The obvious decision, as colleagues, friends, and family kept telling me, was to go to the Caribbean and lead Jade out if its troubles. I would be killing two birds with one stone. It was a guaranteed way for me to recoup the money I'd lost because I knew the space like the back of my hand. And I would also be eliminating the headaches it was causing the rest of the company by turning its fortunes around.

That is what everyone thought…except me. I was willing to do anything else but that. People asked me why, and I asked myself the same question sometimes. But every time I considered it, I had the same reaction: an immediate, gut-wrenching revulsion. Despite the many obvious and rational reasons we explored for why I should lead Jade out of its troubles, any small attempt I made to get myself to change my mind were met with a bad taste in my mouth. Getting on a conference call, taking a meeting, or doing any kind of preliminary work for Jade resulted in a very unpleasant physical and mental reaction. My mind, my body, all of me was saying no; telling me that I was done with it.

I tried to rationalize my feelings to myself and others. I said I felt bored of the industry, so predictable and monotonous. I'd done it for so many years since I was almost fresh out of college; it was yesterday's news. I couldn't live in that environment again; it would be like a slow death. But it seemed almost childish how I was prioritizing how something made me feel above how necessary it was. It took me two years to realize what was truly going on.

I could have never imagined the real reason behind my reluctance. After much soul-searching, I discovered that my subconscious mind was afraid of what would happen to my self-image if I failed at Jade. I had just come out of what I perceived as a big failure after my far-reaching attempt to save the world. My mind was already at full capacity trying to process the lessons learned and make sense of how something so negative could have resulted from trying to do good. The last thing I needed was another existential crisis; something that could easily be triggered if I failed at Jade. But why was failing at Jade, specifically, such a sensitive point for me, given that I never feared failure before?

SECRETS OF THE SUBCONSCIOUS MIND

Here is the train of thought that was hidden from me in my subconscious mind; the one that was secretly controlling my reaction. Jade was a company I built only a few years after I graduated college. I turned it into a great success with very little business or life experience. If I were to fail at returning the company to its former glory, it would mean that I had become completely useless, that I could not even do the things I was able to do when I was just a novice. I had never actually thought this through when I needed to make the decision about Jade; it was all in my subconscious mind. All I was conscious of was that I didn't feel it anymore, that it bored me. It is scary how much goes on in our subconscious mind that we are not aware of!

The moment I became aware of these underlying reasons, the bad taste I had about Jade suddenly disappeared. Why? Because I thrive on challenge; that is what I enjoy. I was almost insulted that I was subconsciously shying away from one. This is what happens when your subconscious and conscious minds are at odds. The subconscious will always win, and that's what prevented me from taking over the leadership at Jade for two whole years. It was only when I aligned the conscious with the subconscious in order to reveal and understand the underlying issues I was grappling with that I was able to overcome this obstacle.

While I was running away from Jade, I was contemplating taking over an agricultural company instead and growing it as a way to recoup the money I'd lost. I knew nothing about agriculture at the time and that company was not doing well despite the fact that billions of pounds worth of investments had been poured into it. Even though I had vast experience as a renewable energy expert, my subconscious mind was willing to take a much higher risk of failure doing something I had no experience in rather than utilizing those skills at Jade.

How could that make any sense? Well, according to my subconscious mind, if I failed in agriculture, it wouldn't damage my self-image. I was new to agriculture and most of the other companies in the industry were doing a horrible job too. It was a much bigger risk for me to fail at Jade, taking on a mission I had already accomplished when I was an amateur. And it wasn't a fear that people were going to find out; it was all about being able to look at myself in the mirror. I was blown away by how deep a maze my subconscious mind had gotten lost in and how strong a grip it held on my career decisions, and certainly on other areas of my life as well.

Can you see how our subconscious mind can work against us? In essence, it is trying to protect us, but often, as a result of some short circuiting, it miscalculates the situation and sends us in the wrong direction. Worse, we go in that direction armed with an explanation from our conscious mind that is different from the true, subconscious reasons we are taking those steps! Just like I thought I didn't want to get involved with Jade because I was bored of it, when in reality, my subconscious mind was afraid I would fail. I say my subconscious and not me in this instance because I spent my life thriving in and enjoying high-risk environments. It was such a surprise and so hard to recognize precisely because it was so uncharacteristic of my usual behavior.

Noticing Your Subconscious Fabrications

You need to be very conscious of this phenomenon and how it might impact you. This isn't something that only happens to me; it's an experience that we all share. I highly advise you to revisit things that you were very resistant to or things you were postponing, perhaps even avoiding. You must dive into the fabrications that your subconscious mind may have created to prevent you from participating in that activity or taking that decision. All you consciously know about those experiences is the surface-level excuse that you gave. The equivalent of "I find this boring" in my Jade story. As we know, that was a fabrication; it wasn't the real reason my mind was resistant.

What fabrications have you been telling yourself? Was it:
"I don't have enough time…"
"If only I was younger…I would have…"
"If I only got a fair chance, I would have been able to…"
"I don't have enough energy to take this on…"
"I'm not sure I would be good at that…"

What else are you telling yourself that might be getting in your way? These are all fabrications that provide a convenient justification as to why you shouldn't do something or why you should. Toss those into the trash. Now, think about what other reasons could possibly exist for why you are avoiding something or why you might be too attached to it? Are there unique circumstances that would make failure unbearable? Does it put you in a situation that risks you discovering things about yourself that you did not know before and that you would rather not know? In other words, does it push you into unchartered waters? Are you subconsciously choosing to stay in the safe environment of your current self-image? The reasons why are unique to each of us, so you must think about your own particular fears and traits, even though this phenomenon is universal to all human beings. As you think of possible reasons behind your actions, you must resist the temptation to bat away what feels embarrassing or confusing. Your initial reaction may be, "Of course not, that is so unlike me!" That is your ego getting in the way. I talk at length about the ego and how it poisons us in my first book, *Super Vision*.

When I became aware of my subconscious fabrications, I started revisiting a lot of big questions in my life that I thought I knew the answers to very well. For example, my preferences for certain things and the main motivations I have for doing things. With a fresh perspective, I was surprised by how the same short circuiting existed in so many other areas of my life. I'm so grateful I discovered this and I'm a much healthier person as a result. Imagine you've been driving a car with a malfunctioning gearbox for years; it's obviously been limiting your speed. Except, in this scenario, you didn't realize there was anything wrong; you simply assumed that this was the top speed of the car. Once you can see the problem and you make it a priority to address it, you can access higher speeds and smoother rides. Similarly, we can truly thrive once we discover the faulty pathways of our subconscious mind. We must deeply examine the destiny we think we have chosen for ourselves. We might be surprised to find that we chose it for the wrong reasons, or even worse, that it was not of our own choosing.

TWO

LIVING IN WONDERLAND

The greatest deception men suffer is from their own opinions.
—JEAN-JACQUES ROUSSEAU

The subconscious fabrications we discussed in chapter 1 can have a profound effect on us. We can find ourselves living in wonderland, sinking into the realm of possibility. I mean that we find ourselves fantasizing about what our lives could have been like if only we "didn't miss the train." Stuck in wonderland, we can only dream about lost opportunities rather than seeing what we are still able to do in the here and now.

Let's return to some of those fabrications. Do you remember a time when you said something like the following?

"If only I was younger, I could have become a great tennis player."
"If only I wasn't always so busy at work, I would have gotten married and started a family."
"If only I was younger, I would have done these hobbies…"
"If only I'd had more support, I would have started my own company."

"If I only had time, I would have pursued this hobby."

"If only I'd had more savings, I would have gone to graduate school."

These sorts of thoughts are usually associated with something you wanted to do or wished you could have done. Instead of actually embarking on doing them or taking any concrete planning steps, our minds subconsciously put a stop to any real hope these wishes can materialize by fabricating a necessary requisite that can never be achieved. For instance, consider the "If only I was younger, I would have done these hobbies…" scenario. In reality, you can't get any younger, so your mind has framed things in a way that puts an end to this ambition altogether. *There is no point in trying this hobby because I can't make myself any younger. It's not up to me really. I would have tried it, but I just don't have a time machine.* This prevents us from moving forward with this goal; we can only fantasize about it in wonderland, in the realm of possibility. These are commonly 'if' statements. It would have only been possible *if* I was younger or *if* I was born into a rich family, and so on.

So, what does our subconscious mind accomplish by forcing us into this train of thought? Well, a lot of things could happen by taking on a completely new activity late in life. You could embarrass yourself by being really bad at it. This is especially true if such statements are made with an air of superiority. For example, "I would have made a terrific tennis player, if only I was younger…" If you took on this challenge at a later age, you might be surprised to discover that you don't actually have any natural talent for it, which might be painful to accept. Thus, to avoid such disappointment, our subconscious mind prevents us from actually finding out by keeping it a fantasy in the realm of possibility.

We must be conscious of these statements. When we hear ourselves saying something in the form of: "If only I had X, I would have done Y," or, "If only I was A, I would have done B," it should act as a warning signal. We should become aware of the feelings building in our subconscious— our fear of failure and our unwillingness to find out whether we will fail or not. Over time, you may recognize that we all make these statements often; we might even say them with a sense of pride, sometimes even with a smile. "If only…I would…" They seem harmless, almost poetic and bittersweet, but they are actually very unhealthy for us.

Our Subconscious May Be Lying to Us

Critically, our subconscious mind can be wrong. We must not be fearful of failure. Failure is the best teacher we have. It tells us what doesn't work and what is not good enough. It is a guiding light; our hidden compass. It is a station that we must go through on our way to our final destination of success. Perhaps we fear failure so keenly because when we look at other people's success and it makes us think less of ourselves when we imagine the possibility of failing. But these people didn't succeed straight away, no one ever does. You just didn't happen to be present during their failures. Failure is an essential prerequisite to success. As long as you gave your best effort, there is no shame in failure. The only shame that lies in failure is the failure to try.

So, what should we do when our subconscious tells us something isn't possible? We must reconsider. We must question ourselves. Why is it not possible to pursue our dreams right now? How robust is our justification for not trying at all? It's true that we can't change our age, how much money we might have, or the family or country we were born into. But, if we are truly serious about a dream, and we objectively determined that pursuing it would greatly benefit our well-being, then we should consider giving it a shot regardless. Yes, it would have been much easier if we had the theoretical advantage of being younger or wealthier, etc. But any situation could have started from a better foundation. We can always dream up more 'perfect' scenarios where we are more prepared.

Instead, we must realize that wherever we are now, there is always a path to where we want to go. That path might be longer than we wanted, depending on our current situation, but that doesn't mean it's a destination we cannot reach; it should not stay merely in the realm of possibility.

When I was in high school, I played many sports competitively. My coaches quickly recognized my fighting spirit—it was why I could excel in almost any sport I played. Many of them spoke with conviction that I would become a world champion one day, if I stayed in the sport. But as I neared my last year of high school, I decided I wanted more from life than that. My ambitions blew up in size. I wanted to transform the economy of the country, to bring radical social and technological change to the world. After I got a full scholarship to MIT, I consciously let go of my athletic dreams to live much bigger ones.

One of the sports I played competitively was squash. A few years into college, a squash world championship was being hosted close by. It was a very heavy moment of realization. Here I am, still a student, and other people my age are competing for the world championship. That could've been me. *If only* I had spent the last three years training in squash instead of focusing on my studies, *I could have become world champion.* I looked at it like it was something that could never happen, and I lamented that

I couldn't get those three years back. But I was still twenty at the time. I could have easily started training again and by twenty-three I could have been world champion. And that is the danger of those statements, of leaving things in wonderland. It prevents you from actually doing the things you dream of while it is still possible!

You can see the tricks that our minds play on us. If I was saying, "I wish I was younger" while I was in college, it's clear that my subconscious was not to be trusted. Now I look back and I say, "You *were* young enough!" Of course, it's hard to recognize that in that moment and that's why you need to take this framework to heart.

It Might Be Hard, but It's Not Impossible

Here's a good habit to develop whenever you catch yourself about to make such statements. Ask yourself, "Do I really want this?" If the answer is yes, then find a way to do it now. If you don't really want it, then don't allow yourself to indulge in the synthetic mental glory of achieving something in another life given the 'right' circumstances. You can never validate whether you would have been able to do it or not. The only way to validate that dream is to do it in the present.

We often think that *if we only* had more—more skills to draw on, or more money in the bank, or more confidence—then we would be ready to pursue what we really want. But as we've discussed, regardless of where you are in life, you could always have more. The key is to craft a plan to get to where you want that is customized to take account of the limited tools and resources that you currently have. The plan will take longer to execute than the virtual plan that comes with youth or money, but, if grounded in reality, it can still work!

What kind of wishful statements have you been making recently? What dreams and wishes do you have that you tend to leave stagnating in the realm of possibility? Write them down. Why have you not embarked on them? These might not be legitimate reasons. If you heard of someone else in your exact circumstances who actually decided to take the leap and pursue the same dreams you were making excuses about, would you judge them? Would you think they'd made a mistake? Probably not. You would probably reflect that it might be hard but it's not impossible. Think about those dreams and wishes; do you still want them? If so, get serious about them. Do they mean enough to you that you would enjoy pursuing them regardless of how things turn out at the end? If yes, do it! If not, then step out of wonderland, because it prevents us from experiencing the pleasures of real life.

We should not write off our dreams as impossible fantasies, only to be enjoyed while reflecting on what could have been. We can't let our chance at achieving them voluntarily slip through our hands. To rewrite our destiny, we must deny ourselves the pleasure of fantasies and embrace what needs to happen in order to make them a reality.

THREE

THE DESIRE TO BE RECOGNIZED

The reward for our work is not what we get, but what we become.
—PAULO COELHO

There are many desires that live within us. Some of them conflict with each other. As a result of this scattered will, we end up wasting a lot of time. The unstoppable human is the one who can align all of their desires in one direction and eliminate the desires that take them in opposite directions. This does not mean we have to go after only one goal; we have too many responsibilities for this to be practical, whether it's family, career, health, community, or personal interests. Instead, it is about channeling the desire to have one ethos, identity or archetype which reflects and aligns with the different responsibilities we have chosen in our life.

For example, take the ethos of wanting to be a force for good in the world. Any decision that you are thinking about can simply be screened with a simple question: "Is this good?" I'm about to respond to someone with a nasty message. Even if they deserve it, is this good? No. Then I won't send the message. Some family members have been asking me to visit them over and over again. Is it good to continue to ignore them because I'm busy? No, they must need me. I'm at a party and there is a lot of alcohol. Everyone is drinking too much. Should I do the same? It's not going to be good for my health or how I'll feel when I wake up tomorrow. Instead, a couple of drinks may just be enough as I socialize. Day-to-day, all the decisions and questions you have can be vetted through the ethos that you have chosen by asking those questions. Is it good for me? Is it good for others? Is it good for the world? Is it good for my future self?

However, there is one desire that is harder to resist than most others: the desire to be recognized. The problem is that it is disguised as a good desire. Let's say you have decided that you want to be a force for good in the world. You probably feel that you want to be recognized for being a force for good. If you are being recognized for it, then you must be living up to your commitments, so it aligns with your goals. That is the trap our subconscious mind falls into.

Sabotaged by Our Thirst for Recognition

Once the desire to be recognized gets a grip on us, it starts polluting our mind and our well-being. Getting that recognition becomes a separate goal that can conflict with your initial goal of being a force for good. Significant amounts of time and possibly even money ends up being spent on getting that recognition. This is time and money that could have been spent directly on the primary goal.

Let's take a simple example. You have been working on an athletic goal, whether it is losing weight, building muscle, or performing a sport at a top level. Having made a lot of progress, you feel the desire to be recognized. So, you post about it on social media. It takes a long time to create that post because you want to present the best image of yourself. Then, after posting, you spend a lot of time—and I mean hours according to your screentime data—checking how people have responded to your post. You analyze and reflect on how much recognition you received; how many views, likes, and comments. Does this sound familiar?

Once the desire for recognition takes over, and it can easily do that if we are not on guard, we start working for people rather than ourselves. We subconsciously become so obsessed with being recognized by them and wanting them to associate us with the values that matter most to us that we allow our mood and well-being to become prisoners of their opinions. In the social media example, for instance, the moment we do not get enough likes we may feel that we have not done enough to reach our goal, and consequently, we don't feel as good.

Outside of social media, think about all the money you spend that you could have saved if it wasn't for the subconscious desire to be recognized. The higher price for the car you need to buy to be recognized as having a certain status. The more expensive house, the designer brands, and the exclusive restaurants, etc. The reality is that a cheaper car, a less expensive home address, or less flashy clothing without a designer logo may be more suitable for us. But they wouldn't have fulfilled our desire to be recognized. Imagine how much money and time we could spend on the things that actually matter to us, that we actually want to do, if the desire to be recognized wasn't taking so much space in our lives.

When we start being conscious of the harmful effects of spending too much time on social media or spending too much money when there is no clear necessity, we might try to cut down. Unfortunately, this doesn't always work because our desire to be recognized is still lurking behind our habits. We must go straight to the monster beneath the symptoms. If we don't face that monster and defeat it, we can't make any significant or consistent progress.

The seeds that are sown in our subconscious mind by the desire to be recognized grow into a need to satisfy other people's expectations. After all, we cannot be recognized by people if we do not live up to or exceed their expectations. That impulse, unfortunately, turns into mental slavery because if we do not get the recognition we crave, we suffer. It is such a vulnerable situation to be in, placing our well-being, self-esteem, and happiness at the mercy of other people's opinions. Yet we do it all the time. You can see now why we need to discard this desire to be recognized. Once it takes root, it shares a quality with our ego; they are both invisible and equally dangerous.

DISCARDING OUR DESIRE TO BE RECOGNIZED

So, how do we discard our desire to be recognized? We must start by disillusioning ourselves of our initial impression that it is a good thing. It feels like validation to be recognized for the things we value and so we feel as if we must have done something right. But we've discussed in detail how harmful this is for us. The minute we feel a desire to be recognized, alarm bells should go off; we must see that urge as poison sold as medicine and immediately deny the thought. Instead, in that instant, we should immerse ourselves in an activity that represents the ethos we originally wanted to be recognized for. So, if we want to be recognized for being fit, then we should exercise to recondition our mind toward the impulses that we want it to present us with. By doing this, we are telling our mind, "Don't push me to encourage people to compliment me on the effort I put in at the gym. Instead, push me to go to the gym more often."

There is a soothing peace to be enjoyed when we cast out the desire to be recognized and dedicate all of our senses to enjoying the activities that either bring us joy or reinforce our identity and what we stand for—or both. Ironically, it is when we move toward this mentality that we will find the recognition seamlessly arriving on its own. This is because we'll be focused on putting in the work rather than distracted by seeking recognition for it. Different destinies await us whether we lust for recognition or we are indifferent toward it because we recognize ourselves the sweetness of the fruits of our labor. We must be wise enough to choose the better of these two destinies, for one leads to self-growth and the other leads to self-destruction.

FOUR

THE RIGHT NOT TO LIKE CHOCOLATE

Care about what other people think and you will always be their prisoner.
—Lao Tzu

People have the right not to like chocolate, even if their dislike of something so delicious doesn't make any sense. As a chocolate lover, I can't wrap my head around this idea, even if I try. How could they not like something so tasty? But there is no point in thinking it through. It is not for me to determine. It is everyone's right to decide what they like and what they don't. Even if it doesn't make any sense to me, it is literally none of my business.

It is the same when it comes to people liking us. It's really none of our business if and why they don't like us. "Why? But it's me we are talking about. How come it's none of my business?!" We suddenly get very defensive and agitated when we realize that somebody doesn't like us. Do you know why? Because we subconsciously take the fact that they don't like us as a negative judgment of our value and worth. If *they* don't like me, it means there is something that is not good about me. People's reaction to this realization tends to either be sadness or an attempt to change the other person's mind. "Let me show you how you are wrong. I am very likable!"

LEARNING TO LET GO

The problem here is not that person's opinion or our ability to convey how likable we are. The real problem is how we are taking the fact that someone doesn't like us as a measure of our self-worth. This is as ridiculous as saying chocolate is bad because some people don't like it. Does chocolate have to bend backward to win them over? No! It's their loss that they don't like chocolate. It is the same thing with you. Just because someone doesn't like you, does not mean you are "bad." People make wrong decisions all the time; they might not even know what's best for them. Even so, it is their life and their right to choose what music, food, and activities they like. That includes people as well. It does not bother us as much when we hear that someone does not like our favorite band or sports activity. We understand that it doesn't reduce the value of these things, even if it's a person we care about that dislikes them. But we suddenly crumble if we hear that someone doesn't like us. Did you know there are tens of millions of Americans who don't like chocolate? Let alone others in the rest of the world that can't appreciate this sweet treat. Not because of intolerance. They simply don't like the taste of chocolate. If tens of millions don't like chocolate, isn't it OK to have a fraction of the people that we encounter not like us?

You must remember that people have a right to choose their preferences, just as you have the right to choose yours, and you must recognize these rights. Say it again: recognize their rights. And we all have the right to determine what we like or want without offering any justification to others. You need to apply the same logic when it comes to you and whether people like you or not. As long as we cling to the expectation that everyone should like us, as long as we expect an explanation for why they don't, it will always bother us.

Whenever you feel you are about to become agitated when you realize that someone doesn't like you, simply remember that phrase: recognize their rights. *It is their right and not mine to determine what they like and what they don't. It does not reflect badly on me if they don't like me, just as it doesn't reflect badly on the amazing films, activities and food that they don't like.* When we remember to recognize their (and our own) rights, it helps us to let go of the fear and worry associated with experiencing people not liking us. We should use the same principle to let go of trying to make people like us in the first place. The reason we do that is because we know we will be tormented if they don't like us, so we put in a huge effort upfront to try to avoid such a painful result. But what if we were just ourselves and we stopped trying to control the result? Chocolate doesn't try hard to make people like it. It simply is what it is; those that like it will come, and those that don't like it won't.

By recognizing our right to determine whether we like someone or not, we should be able to put an end to our obsession with making people like us. However, if you need more help, you could try this exercise. Remember that when people reject you, they are not rejecting all of you. They are rejecting only a part of you. That part might mean a lot to them, but it might not mean as much to you. For instance, you might go on a date and find that after they see the average car that you're driving they become less interested in you. Maybe wealth is something that's very important for them, but it might be inconsequential to you.

People usually frame this sort of behavior very negatively and call such people gold diggers. But what if your date experienced poverty in their childhood and subsequently found themselves attracted to wealth and repulsed by anything that reminded them of those hard times? I'm not saying this explains everyone you would brand as a gold digger. What I am saying is that it's not your business to have to bother with the reasons behind why people don't like you. You don't need to get into the deep dark forests of their subconscious minds to find an explanation that will put your anxieties to rest. Just accept that any explanation will probably have more to do with them than you.

When we recognize that people are only rejecting a part of us, it's a valuable lesson in how to make connections too. A part of us might mean nothing to one person and the whole world to another. You simply need to find those people that appreciate the same human qualities that you do and the parts of yourself that are most important to you. This is the same approach that you would take when choosing people to spend time with—finding those that enjoy the same sports, TV shows, music, etc. You just need to realize that this extends to choosing people too. Instead of trying to convince someone that you are good for them by pursuing them when it's not working, try to move on to the millions out there who might be naturally attracted to what you already have. This doesn't just apply to romantic relationships; it applies to friends, colleagues at work, and even business partners.

An Exception to the Rule

There is one exception to this. If *everyone* doesn't like you, then there is a different problem here we need to address. By everyone, I mean all of the people you go to school or college with, or everyone at work. If everyone doesn't like you except your mom, then yes, you need to ask yourself why. Because there is probably a core reason, a common denominator, and it's probably something that you can easily fix once you are conscious of it. You may have poor hygiene; just shower every day and use a sweat control product. Maybe you are very self-centered, a radical narcissist, and never considerate of other people, so nobody likes to be around you. Once you have found the reason your friends and acquaintances have exiled you, it becomes possible to change the situation.

This happened to me in my childhood. I suddenly woke up and realized I had lost all of my friends. I later realized it was because I'd become very self-centered. I was like a child version of Louis XIV, the French king who famously said in 1655, "L'Etat, c'est moi," which is French for, "I am the state." He was called the Sun King because he thought that France revolved around him. He chose the sun as his royal emblem because he imagined himself to be the light radiating greatness. The moment I realized that this is why people had been distancing themselves from me was the same moment my character changed for the better during that young period of my life.

Let me stress that you should only undergo this sort of deep analysis in the extreme situation where the vast majority of people you know don't like you. Most people are suffering because a handful of people don't like them; they just happen to be the people that we really wanted to like us.

Tools to Change Your Mindset

You are probably thinking this is easier said than done, that you are feeling chained to that person and you can't let go of your desire to be with them. But this just stems from your desire to have them like you back. That takes us back to what we discussed in chapter 3, about our desire to be recognized. The desire for recognition turns you into a slave. It takes away your freedom. You have to work for the person you want to be recognized by, and you might resort to pretending to be things you are not—to lie, in effect—just to get their recognition.

> Say these mantras in your head:
> You don't have to like me.
> I don't have to live up to your expectations.
> I prefer to live my own…

That chained feeling is also caused by the subconscious thought that you have been rejected, which makes you feel unworthy. Feeling rejected doesn't feel good, and your subconscious mind doesn't like it. It tells you that the only way to take that bad feeling away is for that person to change their mind and realize how good you are. The ego is at play here, in a very subtle way, in the subconscious trenches of your mind. If you stop framing what you experienced as a *rejection*, you won't feel the need to vie for someone's approval. Once you update the settings in your subconscious mind, that chained feeling to the person will disappear. You can update those settings by changing your thoughts to ones that reflect a high level of emotional intelligence. Let's go back over these three thoughts again:

Thought 1: I recognize their rights.

Everyone has the right to determine what they like and what they don't. They might not like some of the best films or songs ever made, but their opinion doesn't make those things any less valuable. *If they don't like me, that is their right; it is none of my business and it does not change my self-worth.*

You can never be free if you are afraid to be disliked. You don't need a high level of confidence and you don't need a lot of amazing qualities. All you need is to remember their right to choose what they like. *Whose right is it to decide whether they like me or not? Not me!* If you start saying things like, "But what did I do? I was so nice to them. Maybe I didn't get a chance to show them the rest of me," then you are infringing on their rights. Let go of the heavy load you carry around that comes from wanting people to like you.

Thought 2: They are not rejecting all of me; they are only rejecting part of me.

Nobody has everything. You are bound to meet people who value a certain quality that you don't have. It's pointless to try to build a bond that would take so much effort because you fundamentally lack what they value most. Instead, you can build a long-lasting bond with someone that is naturally attracted to the qualities you already have.

Thought 3: I only pursue people who like what I represent.

You can't feel hurt if you get rejected by someone you weren't pursuing in the first place. You won't even notice you were rejected. Once you stop pursing people who do not like what you represent, you will never be rejected. At least within your own frame of reference. When you realize that you are attracted to someone that appreciates very different qualities from the ones you have, it's important to pull on the brakes. It could also apply in the workplace when you are recruiting someone who you think has terrific pedigree, but who you instinctively feel doesn't want to work at your company because you or your company represent different things from what they are attracted to. In these circumstances, you don't have to feel rejected or see it as a challenge to make them change their mind if there is a misalignment in goals and values.

We can rewrite our destiny and experience a much lighter and more enjoyable life if we can develop an indifference to being disliked. Such indifference only comes with practice.

FIVE

CHANGE THE PAST

Before you heal someone, ask him if he's willing to give up the things that make him sick.

—Hippocrates

What a strange prospect. Can I really change the past? How...? The past is simply a record of memories that you have kept of a period of time that has passed. But that record is not necessarily accurate. What you remember might have never happened. That's because what you remember is your perception, not the reality, and those can be completely different. Perception vs. reality is the main theme of my first book, *Super Vision*. It's an education that every individual must undergo if they aspire to remain sharp, fruitful and happy.

Imagine you went to an event that you've never been to before. It's attended by a crowd of people very different from the ones you usually hang out with. Afterward, your memory of it is that people were looking at you in a strange way, like you didn't belong there. You start wondering if your clothing was not up to standard or whether it was to do with the way you look. Feelings of inferiority creep up on you and you never go to that event again. In reality, they might have been looking at you in an intrigued way as opposed to a disrespectful way. They might have been thinking, "Who is that person that I've never seen before?" But your low self-esteem at the time might have encouraged you to perceive any unusual attention you were getting as evidence that there must be something wrong with you. The past that you created for yourself may have never existed.

So many people are trapped in the past in this way. Held back by memories of bad experiences and the psychological damage it has inflicted on them. The good news is you don't have to continue to be shackled by such memories. Why? Because it's in the past, and the past, or your memory of it, might have never happened. You are not suffering because of what happened in the past; you are suffering because of the meaning that you are attributing to what happened in the past.

For instance, let's take quite an extreme example. A woman finds out that her husband has been cheating on her. This looks like a traumatizing experience at first glance. But the truth is, it's only traumatizing if you want it to be. She would likely be traumatized by the meaning she has attached to the experience rather than the experience itself. Her initial reaction might include self-berating thoughts such as: "My husband is cheating on me because I'm not good enough," or, "I'm clearly not worthy of love or even respect. Otherwise, why would he dare to commit such a heinous act!" Other thoughts might focus on a feeling of doom, "I'm destroyed because my marriage is ruined." But it is these thoughts themselves that are the traumatizing event. It's her conclusion that her life is destroyed that will subconsciously lead her to destroying herself emotionally.

Trauma is experienced as an emotional reaction to a horrible incident. It is common to experience shock and denial initially, but more complicated and sustained long-term emotional reactions can develop as a result of trauma. It can also lead to physical symptoms such as headaches, illness, and disease. All the more reason to fight against the debilitating symptoms it wreaks on our bodies and minds. There lies an alternative. You can experience a horrible betrayal and not allow it to destroy you.

TAKING BACK CONTROL OF OUR PAST

Most mental health practitioners, when they define and attempt to heal trauma, are oblivious to the fact that it does not come about from the events themselves but from the meaning we have attached to such events. Yes, it is natural when experiencing betrayal to attach some pretty negative meanings to it. But, over time, it's possible to recognize that we are in control of what meaning we assign to the situation. And, consequently, we can gain back control of our past.

During such a painful event, it might be difficult to generate alternative thoughts; this requires a very strong mind. But, with time, it is certainly possible to develop our ability to assign more "correct" and positive thoughts to events as they unfold before us. By "correct" thoughts, I mean thoughts that are healthy for us. This might sound extremely hard to do because romantic betrayal is an extreme example that doesn't happen every day. But it's a strong medicine with even stronger results. Alternative thoughts that could have been assigned to the same event include: "I was apparently married to someone who had very different ethical values to those that are most important to me," and, "I'm glad these circumstances were able to remove the mask he wore so that I could realize who he truly was and not waste any more of my life living a lie."

Only the most well-trained minds can deflect negative thoughts in real time as events that are hard to bear unfold. The good news is you *can* train your mind to be like that. But don't aim to be a black belt on the first day. Make it a lifelong mission; something you will get better at with time. Recall that almost all of us not only struggle to manage our reactions in real time, but also allow those faulty emotional reactions to plague us for a long time after the event has passed, leading to long-term trauma. If you can't manage your thoughts and emotional reactions in real time, start by training yourself to review them after the event has passed. Ensure you correct them so you are not responsible for your own misery by clinging to negative perceptions that damage your self-image and self-worth..

Let's demonstrate this using a less extreme example. In a meeting, one of your colleagues said something that felt disrespectful to you. You ended up having a very bad memory of that meeting, not because of what actually happened but because of how you have recorded the memory. Instead of feeling disrespected and taking on the damage yourself, you could instead feel pity for them. They must be envious of you, or they might not have manners or business etiquette. They might be going through a painful experience that is clouding their judgment or causing them to say hurtful things. In all these cases, you did not process what happened as a negative reflection on yourself and your self-worth. And you might be able to do that in real time in this instance because it's much easier to process than a betrayal. You obviously still have the right to take any action you want, whether it is standing up for yourself during the meeting, confronting them afterward, or reporting them. But here I'm focusing on how we can mentally process the event.

With more extreme events, such as walking into your own bedroom to discover your husband or wife betraying you, most people might not be able to maintain such a sharp and mature lens in real time when it comes to what interpretation they choose to give to the event. This is because it is such a shocking and extreme experience, although it's still theoretically possible to maintain the sharp lens of perception, though less likely. This line of thought could be extended to other extreme events such as war, death, abuse, rape, etc. So, what do we do about such extreme events?

A Second Chance to Change the Story

We still get a second chance. We can always change the past. Remember that the past is simply a record of feelings, thoughts, and meanings that we have assigned to a certain event or memory. Change those meanings in the record and you change the memory and the past with it. Let's elaborate using a lighter example. Can you remember a time when you went with a few friends on a trip? Perhaps it was a great trip for them but not for you? Perhaps that's obvious in the way you each reminisce about it? They talk about how the sun was shining and how much they loved catching up with each other after so long apart. You only recall that you weren't able to get into that museum that you'd planned to visit and that you got overcharged for your meal. How come? It was the same trip wasn't it? How could the same thing be good and bad at the same time? It is because each of you assigned different thoughts, feelings and meanings to the same thing and you can still assign different thoughts, feeling and meanings years later. You can "change" the trip even though it's in the past. It might be the same hotel, the same restaurants, and the same people present, but your perception of what happened can be altered and so, in time, will your memory of it.

The power of changing the meaning we attribute to the past is astonishing. By choosing to change our thoughts, we can remove major obstacles that were hindering us from moving forward. Perhaps we are still stuck in the past, trying to overcome something that we can't go back to without a time machine. A past failure is usually associated with a feeling of incompetence and disappointment. Viewed through a healthier lens, it becomes an education. We are now thankful for this failure because of what it taught us. With this shift in our thinking, we have the confidence to try again as opposed to being traumatized and fearful about failing again. Now, when we plan for our second attempt, our thinking changes from: "I will either succeed or I will fail," to, "I will either succeed or I will learn some more."

In a similar way, changing the meanings we attribute to past events can change something as painful as betrayal and the tsunami of painful emotions that come with it into something more positive such as a wake-up call; a realization that perhaps we have been too naïve and that the world we live in is far from ideal. The memory of abuse can be altered to a recognition that we've made the mistake of being too toler-ant. Or perhaps it is not a mistake of our own making but the reality of life. Pain and tragedy are an intrinsic part of living and we can't live a perfect, unscratched existence. We can only choose how to respond to those scratches. The key will always lie in not letting such events lead us to thoughts that destroy our self-image: that is where trauma starts.

Leo Tolstoy, the famous Russian writer, once said something that I like very much: "We lost because we told ourselves we lost." Stop telling yourself that you lost. We now have the superpower to reshuffle the past to suit our current and future needs. We can rewrite our destiny, regardless of what we think has happened previously. It is not the past that determines our present and future. It is the present that determines our past.

SIX

FREUD VS. ADLER

The only real mistake is the one from which we learn nothing.
—Henry Ford

Two of the most prominent figures in the world of psychology are Sigmund Freud and Alfred Adler. You've probably heard Freud's name before, but you're less likely to have heard of Adler who is significantly underrated. Both are Austrian psychologists who have contributed a huge amount to the field of psychology. But a key difference between the two is the importance that they each place on the past.

On one hand, Freud viewed the past as the key that can unlock all the mysteries in your life. He believed that if you are unsure about why someone is behaving in a certain way or is strongly clinging to certain thoughts, you only need to study their past and you will find the answers you are looking for. Freud also believed that all of our fears and traumas that shape how we live today are caused by events that we experienced in the past.

Adler, on the other hand, believed that the past is irrelevant and would go as far to say that the past does not even exist. Adler is likely to agree with everything we discussed in chapter 5 about the past being nothing but a record of thoughts that we associate with events that happened. If he were to read that chapter, I can imagine him smiling and nodding with pride, saying, "Go on, Sherife!" I'm not sure what Freud would say.

So, who's right? Sigmund Freud, the father of modern psychology, who stresses that the past is responsible for everything that we do today? Or the far less famous Alfred Adler who belittled the importance that humans assign to the past to the extent that he denied its existence. If I had to choose between Freud and Adler on this topic, I would definitely choose Sherife.

"What??" You might say.

THE BEST OF BOTH WORLDS

Instead of choosing one school of thought, as most practicing psychologists do when it comes to deciding how to treat their clients, I see the benefit in both approaches. By blending them to create a third approach, as opposed to viewing them as contradictory, there is much more value to be gained.

On one hand, we must recognize that, in many cases, the past *is indeed* the source of our traumas, as Freud insisted. If you are suffering from some type of trauma, emotional pain or severe inclination or bias toward something, it can most likely be explained by certain events or patterns that occurred in your past which led you to this present point of suffering. We should use this approach in order to understand the underlying causes of our habits, beliefs, and preferences as well as the fears that we are experiencing today.

On the other hand, we must not allow these past events to determine our present and future. By recognizing that our traumas were not necessarily a result of the events themselves but rather of the ideas that we have associated with those events, we are able to change these ideas and thus our past. This is why several people can experience the same difficult event but not all of them will become scarred by it in the same way. It's a matter of what thoughts each person has attributed to the same event, and some thoughts are a lot more scarring than others. This could be called mental fitness, but it is not really a sign of strength, as it occurs subconsciously. Think about war, for example. Some soldiers become traumatized by it whereas others do not, despite the fact that they fight the same battles. The distinction is how they perceive and reflect on events. I am traumatized by my misfortunes vs. I am not traumatized despite my misfortunes.

And we should not underestimate the power of mental trauma. It can sometimes hurt more than physical trauma, lasting far longer—for years or decades—if it's not resolved. The advantage of mental trauma, however, is that it only occurs if you allow it. Even if it seems to be outside our control, we do allow it subconsciously. Physical trauma, on the other hand, is often out of our control. If your train collides with another, for instance, you can't prevent it. Physical trauma is almost guaranteed and there's nothing you can do about it. However, after the collision, we have the space to determine which thoughts we want to associate with it. Will we let it traumatize us or will we thrive mentally despite what happened? Most people are unaware that this space even exists and consequently, it is those thoughts that appear, unchecked, that traumatize us. Without this awareness, we cannot determine the direction of our lives. We will simply be dominos that fall as a result of whatever forces act upon us.

By intentionally choosing our own, positive version of the past and ignoring other interpretations, are we living in denial? Not at all. This is not about randomly choosing a reality that happens to be lighter to carry. Instead, we are simply being conscious of the fact that our strong emotions about the past are just a product of the thoughts we chose to attach to certain events. If we made that choice once, we can simply make it again. The first time we made that choice, we did it subconsciously, in a blink of an eye. Today, we can take our time, revisiting those choices and reexamining the level of truth that they actually contain.

We may be surprised to find that there is a plethora of other possibilities when it comes to thoughts that we could associate with the same event. And that the thoughts we had chosen initially might not be the most accurate representation of reality. On the contrary, I actually believe we are living in denial if we *do not* revisit the past. Most likely, we have chosen a very narrow interpretation of what happened and then stubbornly refused to consider anything else.

Finally, I want to make sure that none of the ideas I have expressed here are taken as a criticism of Freud or Adler or the respective schools of psychology that they have founded. These two gentlemen are giants of the world of psychology and I am grateful for the professional contributions that they have both made to humanity throughout their careers.

Instead of choosing to slavishly follow the ideas of one or the other, Freud or Adler, imagine that you have an appointment with each. First comes the meeting with Freud, where you will revisit your past to identify events that were responsible for any situation that you are suffering from today. Once you have identified those events, you move on to your next meeting with Adler. Here you explore the ideas and feelings that you've associated with those past events and determine whether they are accurate or if there could be other more reasonable possibilities that could occupy their place.

We must not allow the past to choose our destiny for us. Armed with a new perspective on the past that once caused us trauma, we can now defeat those traumas and rewrite our destiny. Just don't tell Freud and Adler that you're seeing them both.

PART II

REDESIGN YOUR BRAIN

Our brain controls every process that takes place in our body. There are a million operations that it's running quietly in the background without us even being aware of it. Digestion, muscle repair, and sleep are just a few that we are not actively involved in; we leave it all to our brains. By we, I mean our conscious self. But we have loosened the reins on our brain too much; we have let it run wild, unchecked. To the point that we may have become prisoners of our own minds. It is time to rein in the mind and regain control. It is time to regain consciousness.

_____

SEVEN

HOW OUR THOUGHTS CAN CHANGE REALITY

A remedy made out of a certain leaf...but there was a charm to go with the remedy; and if one uttered the charm at the moment of its application, the remedy made a person perfectly well; but without the charm there was no efficacy in the leaf.

—PLATO

Our medical system has become so advanced today that we can instantly diagnose and treat most illnesses. Whether it's advanced imaging devices and tests that can accurately tell us what is wrong with our body, or sophisticated surgical interventions and medications that can modify our physical structure and alter many chemical reactions in our body, the options on the table are impressive. We enjoy a plethora of medical luxuries that have been developed over the last few decades.

One can only wonder how our ancestors dealt with disease and injury for thousands of years when medical knowledge was so scarce and expertise was isolated in small parts of the world rather than democratically open to everyone. You must have seen a movie capturing one of those strange ancient medical interventions that were common for thousands of years. A typical scene would involve a very sick person lying on a bed after many days of high fever and coughing. A doctor or, more likely, a healer would suddenly be summoned. They would usually pull out some mysterious balm from a magical looking jar or prescribe something extremely unusual like the blood of a young goat or the feces of a rat. Nobody would dare second guess what the healer was prescribing at that time.

Another strange medical solution that was regularly used throughout human history was bloodletting, often to treat depression and mental illness. This involved cutting the patient's skin and draining blood out of them. It was thought, at the time, that having too much blood contributed to illness. Bloodletting was still popular until the nineteenth century!

We might marvel that these strange techniques were ever used as medicine. But the real question is: how could they be used so religiously for thousands of years when we know today that things like bloodletting and rat feces have no scientific basis whatsoever when it comes to their healing properties? The only explanation is they must have worked. If they didn't, people would have simply stopped using these techniques. So, how and why did they work at the time and what has changed today that has stopped their magical properties from being effective?

OUR THOUGHTS CAN CHANGE OUR REALITY

The answer lies in what science now calls *the placebo effect*. Placebos are still widely used by the medical community today. Thankfully, they have evolved from strange things like a young goat's blood to a simple sugar pill. What do sugar pills and ancient magical potions have in common?

They can both result in curing diseases. But how are they responsible for actually helping people recover? The magic of not knowing is at play here. The patient does not know that the magical balm that the healer is using is basically useless. Similarly, they don't know that the pill that their doctor has prescribed is nothing more than sugar.

So how does the placebo effect work? The healing process starts once the patient has felt some relief at the arrival of the doctor and has mentally conditioned themselves that they are about to get better, *because that is what doctors do.* When the doctor prescribes something, many patients feel that the doctor must have figured out what was making them ill and identified the correct remedy that will relieve them of their suffering. The patient now believes that all they need to do is take that medicine and they will start recovering shortly after. Both ancient traditions and modern data have shown that this belief produces recovery for a significant percentage of people.

That is why drinking the fresh blood of a young goat will not heal you today. The average modern person has gone through some level of classical education that undermines the belief in its efficacy. They are resolute that it would be silly to expect a goat's blood to heal an illness. Instead, today, it works with the sugar pill, but only if the patient believes they are receiving genuine medicine.

It is not the sugar pill that has magical properties of course. There is nothing magical about sugar, unless by sugar you mean a freshly-baked, warm chocolate chip cookie! But there is a reason that placebos are so effective: it's the power of our mind. Our brain is so powerful that it has the capacity to reprogram the rest of our body to comply with its wishes. It can order it to recover or to get sick. It's common knowledge that mental health issues can lead to physical illness. The placebo effect shows that the opposite is also possible. Just as your mind can make you physically ill, it can also heal you. What a phenomenal reality. Can a single fact be any more empowering than this? Our thoughts are so powerful that they can even cure us from disease!

EMBRACING THIS HIDDEN POWER

After World War II, Henry Beecher was one of the first doctors to systematically document the positive effect of placebos. In other words, the power of our mind to cure us from pain and disease. In 1955, he published a study that included 1,082 participants undergoing treatments for pain and other ailments. The study showed that 35% of the patients' symptoms were relieved by placebo alone. As an American citizen, Henry Beecher also served in World War II with the US Army. He was stationed in North Africa and Italy throughout the war, where morphine supplies were scarce. One of his most memorable moments was when he noticed a soldier about to undergo an operation being injected with saltwater instead of morphine. However, the soldier thought he was being injected with morphine and didn't show any signs of pain during the operation.

Do you realize the power of your thoughts? They have the ability to uplift you or bury you. Our thoughts are powerful enough to allow us to make miraculous recoveries and demonstrate superhuman abilities like the American soldier we just discussed. If you have the ability to heal your physical symptoms with positive thoughts, then you also have the ability to heal your mental and emotional pain. It's just a case of eliminating the thoughts that have caused them and replacing them with nourishing ones. The negative image that you have of yourself can be turned around. And so can all those bad habits you have been wanting to change.

What you tell yourself, your brain believes, and the rest of your body will fall in line. We must garden our thoughts daily, perhaps even more frequently than that. We must always be conscious of what we are thinking. For we are always either spreading poison or a magic potion throughout our body. Most of us are not even aware of what we are thinking. Our thoughts have become like software running in the background on autopilot, outside our conscious control. As a result, we are not mindful of whether we are pumping poison or nourishment through our system. I would guess that most of us are pumping poison, such as self-defeating thoughts, without even realizing it. That is why we need to become more aware and gradually learn to take control of them through consistent trial and error.

The quality of your thoughts matter. It is what creates your identity and your view of the world. It is what grows in you; what settles and takes control of your reality. If you think you're not very smart, that is what you will become or remain. If you think you're not good at sports, you will never try to get better, and when you actually play, you will do poorly, which will reinforce your initial thoughts. Instead, we must use the various tools available to us to advance. With the right practice and belief systems, one can literally do anything and become anyone. Think: I can and I will.

I should say at this point that I'm in no way saying that real medicine only works through the placebo effect or that it doesn't have any real efficacy. I am certainly not saying that you should ignore medicine and instead only use your brain to heal. I'm also in no way encouraging you to do dangerous experiments such as in the case of the soldier that had an operation without taking morphine! But you must not ignore the vast powers of your brain and the enormous capabilities that lay inside of it, unused, waiting to be harnessed. We might not be where we want in life, but this isn't because of what we lack. It is because we use so little of what we do have.

So, what are your first steps toward embracing these hidden powers? Be aware of your thoughts; choose the ones you want to keep carefully and which ones you must discard. Make sure that they align with your best interests. Now believe in your ability to bring these thoughts to life. Believe with the certainty you have that the sun will set and then rise again each day. When you have put in the consistent work necessary to make these thoughts beliefs and these beliefs part of your identity, they will materialize. All you need now is to clear the doubts and uncertainties in your mind that prevent you from realizing what you want. Cut off your mental chains and reach for that which you desire. Sometimes, just believing what our destiny is or is not is the first step we need to take for that destiny to unfold.

EIGHT

THE PURSUIT OF SUPERIORITY

Don't judge each day by the harvest you reap but by the seeds that you plant.
—ROBERT LOUIS STEVENSON

We've all felt that we aren't good enough at some point. While we may think that we are alone in feeling that way, it is actually a common experience, regardless of our levels of accomplishment or attractiveness. The only difference in how people experience this feeling is its frequency and in what areas of our life we direct that feeling toward.

Today, there are more people than ever regularly experiencing this feeling. It is a self-doubt pandemic, and it's driven by social media. It's easy to feel that you are not good enough when you are bombarded by nonstop pictures and videos of people who are wealthier, better-looking, fitter, and seemingly having more fun than you.

The feeling may be universal, but how we respond to that feeling is certainly not. Most people take a subconscious approach that limits their progress. For example, when it comes to money, our self-image could easily be affected when we are surrounded by people on social media who are much wealthier than us. One way we justify this *inferiority* that we feel is by excusing it. *I was not born into a wealthy family*, we think, *and that's why I'm not rich like them.* The constant pain of comparison means we eventually demote our self-image and create a rationale that justifies our limitations.

The problem this creates is twofold. First, the feeling of inferiority lingers. We continue to recognize that we lack something in a way that is not healthy and doesn't make us feel whole. Secondly, we prevent ourselves from building on that which we lack because in justifying why those gaps exist, we are accepting the status quo as unchangeable: *I cannot choose what kind of family I'm born into and that is what determines my wealth.* That is the subconscious train of thought that occurs in our minds, instead of realizing that we can do something about it.

Let's consider another example. You go to a birthday party and you are surprised by how many people are there. Perhaps you think about how the birthday boy or girl must have many more friends and acquaintances than you do. That negatively affects our self-image and so we proceed to solidify that position by subconsciously creating a justification for it. In this case, we might say to ourselves that we went to a small high school where we didn't have a lot of people in our class. If we went to a bigger high school, like our friend did, we would have had a much bigger circle of friends. And that circle would have grown even bigger through the friends of those friends that we would get introduced to with time.

The justifications we create for ourselves differ from person to person. But the process we use and the results we end up with are the same. Ultimately, we end up not feeling good about ourselves and we accept those feelings and the inferior self-image that comes with them as something that is permanent and out of our hands. We decide that we have to simply accept it. With time, this could develop into an inferiority complex. This is a condition that occurs when we constantly have doubts about our abilities, whether they are true or not. Some people might actually have superior abilities to most, but they are still plagued by feelings they are not good enough in almost every situation.

On the other hand, if someone does have inferior abilities to most, you might ask the question: Is it not *natural* that they would feel inferior to people? Is this really an inferiority complex or just a solid understanding of their reality?

Well, no.

But why? Because those with an inferiority complex, whether justified or not, are stuck in that cycle of self-doubt and unable to make progress. There is an alternative response to a realization of your own inferiority relative to others: to get better.

Turning our Inferiority Complex into an Edge

As I said earlier, while the feeling of not being good enough is universal, the way we respond to it is not. So far, we have discussed the way most people subconsciously respond to such feelings of inferiority which ultimately develops into an inferiority complex. The other way to respond to these same feelings of inferiority is what is known as the pursuit of superiority.

Alfred Adler was a big proponent of the pursuit of superiority. Simply put, it is wanting to get better at something that you are not good at and actually working toward that goal. An inferiority complex and the pursuit of superiority both start with an unpopular realization: that we suck at something. But how we process this realization is completely different depending on the pathway we subconsciously choose. If we choose the pursuit of superiority, after we become conscious of what we are not good at, we decide to get better at it, to put in the work and the long-term commitment. Results take time though. Sometimes, people take on the pursuit of superiority route only to switch, halfway, developing an inferiority complex. This is because it takes too much effort to achieve the results they were hoping for and this triggers feelings of shame around being a slow learner. Indeed, it's easy to fall into the trap of finding comfort in our inferiority complex. By seeing our limitations as beyond our control, we relinquish the weight of responsibility and avoid the need to do anything about it.

Instead, what if we turn our inferiority complex into an inferiority edge? Knowing that we lack something or aren't good enough at it can become a motivator if it is followed up by the will and action to change the situation and improve. This will set us apart from others who are not conscious of their shortcomings and perhaps think too highly of themselves to consider that they could improve. Our inferiority edge propels us past these people because we put the work in every day to get better while they remain in the same place.

One does not have to see results today to feel good about oneself. It is sometimes sufficient to recognize one's efforts without yet seeing the results. Give yourself credit that you still have the will to get better; that you have put in the work today when you could have done nothing; that you are not just mindlessly following a routine like a zombie but are paying close attention to your progress; that you are making any necessary changes to your process that will keep you on course. Give yourself credit for the positive actions you have taken; it will help you sustain these actions and turn them into regular habits. Consistency is the only pathway to long-term results.

In the example we discussed above of not having as many friends as your acquaintance, you can either find justifications that allow you to bury the matter or you can be proactive about it. In this case, if you did not get a chance to build a community around you back in high school, you can still do it today. You can choose to create another community for yourself if you make it a priority. You might choose a hobby, for example, and join a group of athletes, dancers, or book enthusiasts. We must realize that important things take time to build, especially when it comes to human relationships. If it matters to you, persevere, and do not allow setbacks to undermine your will or interest.

In the example about money, instead of finding justification for our financial situation, we can take steps to acquire wealth. This is also a long-term process. But it's worth thinking it through thoroughly first. Ask yourself *why* you want to make more money. Is it because there is a genuine need for it? Or is it because you think that money will make you look successful in the eyes of others? Chasing money for the wrong reasons can be a waste of time and we might be surprised by how fleeting the joy is that it provides once we finally have it in our hands.

We might feel that our weaknesses are set in stone, but we can rewrite the destiny we feel we were born into. We must not let our feelings of inferiority fracture our self-image, but rather use it as an advantage to fuel our motivation. In the pursuit of superiority, we can still succeed, regardless of where we are right now. We must only recognize that we don't have to remain in our current reality. By planning our journey to a different destination and taking small and consistent steps every day, we will eventually, with patience, arrive at our chosen destiny. Sometimes it might feel like our best isn't good enough. But that doesn't mean that we can't get better.

NINE

WHAT I LEARNED
FROM KILLING VAMPIRES

More is lost by indecision than wrong decision. Indecision is the thief of opportunity.

—CICERO

One time, a mouse came into my grandmother's apartment. It was my fault; I had left the window in the laundry room open for a few days without realizing it. Mr. Mouse was apparently walking by outside the open window and saw that a gateway had suddenly appeared which might lead to a world of rewards. The second I saw him I realized all of this. I also realized another thing: I needed to get him out ASAP. A mouse in Grandma's house was not a great idea.

Mr. Mouse made his way into the kitchen. *That's right where I need you,* I thought, *in a confined space where I can catch you.* I proceeded to pick up a broom and a bucket. I had an additional challenge to juggle within my task. I didn't want to kill Mr. Mouse; I just wanted him out of the house. My plan was to scoop him into the bucket and toss him out onto the street. Why would I want to kill him? He hadn't done anything wrong; he was just carrying on with his life like I was. That was my rationale for not killing all kinds of organisms; even the ones that look repulsive or are regarded as fair targets by most, like spiders or flies.

It didn't turn out to be easy. Mr. Mouse didn't want to get into the bucket. I chased him around the kitchen for half an hour. I even spoke to him. *"I'm not trying to kill you! I won't hurt you. Just get into the bucket and I'll put you back on the street."* I imagined myself in Mr. Mouse's head for a second. That was when I realized what the problem must be. He must have been close to having a heart attack. He was probably thinking, *"This giant human is out to kill me."* Thirty minutes of being chased to death can be an awfully long and traumatic time for a mouse. Suffice to say, my plan wasn't working.

I didn't tell my family because I didn't want anyone to panic or object to my perhaps controversial respect of Mr. Mouse's right to live. So, I called some friends. Their ideas ranged from just smashing him with the broom to giving him poison or setting a mouse trap. All of these were off the table for me. Then, in a magical flash of realization, I got an idea. I will get Mr. Mouse drunk. Then, after he passes out, I'll just sweep him into the bucket and toss him back onto the street. Even if he doesn't pass out, he will be disoriented enough that I can catch him easily.

I used to collect rare single malt whisky at the time and I must have left one at my grandma's house for some reason—a bottle of Glenmorangie. The only other alcohol I found was wine, but I felt it might be too weak to do the trick. As hesitant as I was to waste some really good single malt on Mr. Mouse, there seemed to be no other option. Besides, it was just a sip. So, I poured some whisky into a plastic bottle cap, left it on the kitchen floor, closed the door on my way out, and waited for him to take the bait.

I gave Mr. Mouse a few hours to feel safe enough to come out from under the oven where he was hiding and sniff the new, rich smell of fine single malt that must have started to tease his nostrils. And indeed, a few hours later, I knew Mr. Mouse had partaken. I started hearing some loud noises as if all the pans in the kitchen were suddenly falling on the floor. Mr. Mouse was clearly drunk and high on energy from the alcohol; he was running around the kitchen and crashing into the cupboards, disoriented. He was the mouse version of Captain Jack Sparrow from Pirates of the Caribbean.

I waited for the noise to die down and then I opened the kitchen door. Sure enough, Mr. Mouse was lying on his back with a full belly, drunk on my finest whisky. I immediately scooped him into the bucket with a broom and tossed him onto the street. I never did say anything to my family. But I was proud of myself. Given how much time the whole thing took, I made sure to never open the laundry room window again.

VAMPIRE HUNTER

There's one exception to my utilitarian respect of all organisms I encounter. Mosquitoes. Why do I discriminate against mosquitoes? I think it's mainly because if I left them in the room, they would happily suck my blood while I slept. Even if I told them not to, they wouldn't listen to me, and I would wake up with plenty of marks on my body. Evidence that they spent the night feasting on me. Not to mention the often painful bites which aren't pretty. I think that sums up my disregard for mosquito life.

I encounter mosquitoes often because I love nature. Lakes, rivers, seas. I like to have one nearby as often as I can. Me and mosquitoes have that in common; we both like to be around water. It's common, therefore, to find me standing on the bed holding one slipper in each hand, playing Rambo against the mosquitoes. I've learned to tolerate them more in recent years, but there are times when I've spent an hour or more in a bar fight with them after being woken by their attempts to bite me. I'd hear the high-pitched whine they'd make as they dived from the ceiling toward me on the bed. It reminded me of the haunting sound World War I fighter jets used to make.

I've developed so many techniques for killing mosquitoes over the years with nothing more than my slippers. I've even developed names for them: the boomerang, the mummy, the light trap, etc. *"That's a lot of time and effort on murdering mosquitoes,"* you might say. You're right. But there is at least one valuable life lesson that's emerged from this experience. Often, as I spot my mosquito target sitting on a wall, I would approach it very slowly, raising my arm and placing my elbow at the perfect angle, allowing me to hit it with the highest speed possible, like a catapult. The problem is, sometimes, as a result of taking too much time to find the perfect angle and position, the mosquito flies away just a split second before I'm about to swing. It goes and hides somewhere else and, often, I don't find it again. The opportunity is lost forever.

OUR MISSED OPPORTUNITIES

I realized I made the same mistake in life. Many of us do. I've had important opportunities in the past where I took my sweet time to make a move. By the time I was ready, the opportunity was gone. I wasn't taking my time out of laziness but rather to ensure I was well-prepared, motivated by a desire to really nail that opportunity in the best way possible. I would wait for the perfect angle, and that angle always seemed to be just minutes away from perfectly locking in on the target. Inevitably, the target would suddenly disappear on many occasions, and I would lose my shot.

I'm sure this has happened to you too. Have you ever found yourself admiring a speaker at a conference as they delivered their speech on stage? After their presentation, you see them standing across the room, surrounded by other people. Instead of going and joining the queue to talk to them, you might think, *Let me wait until they are standing alone… then I'll go over.* Five minutes later, you look around for the speaker, and you can't find them anywhere. They simply finished their session and left. A missed opportunity.

The same happens in our personal relationships. Perhaps you are at a bar and you notice a person that intrigues you. You make eye contact and exchange a few glances throughout the night, but you don't go and talk to them. You tell yourself that you will go and speak to them later. Again, to your surprise, they end up leaving shortly after with their friends. You'll never know what could have been because you didn't try.

Similarly, when we want to discuss important topics with the people we are closest to, we often put it off, waiting for the "right time." We keep waiting for the moment to arise or we come up with reasons why *now* is not a good time or why *later* would be a better time. As the days drag on, that moment never comes and we end up looking back and wishing that we had had that conversation earlier. Perhaps the situation got much morse, or the person we want to speak to isn't with us on this planet any more. We thought we would have time to do it later.

Likewise, a soccer player is sprinting with the ball toward the goal during the last few minutes of the World Cup final. He has a great opportunity to score and win for his country. His opponent almost catches up with him as he bears down on the keeper. Now is the time to shoot. But he doesn't shoot. He doesn't feel certain that he will score, so he decides to continue moving forward, hoping he will find a better angle, only to realize that he was in a better place three seconds ago. Realizing that his chance is now worsening with time, he panics and shoots. He misses.

Sometimes we need to realize that just because a shot *could be better,* doesn't mean that we will get a better opportunity to make it. Instead of waiting for the perfect shot, we have to train ourselves to recognize when it's *good enough* to take. The reality is that perfect shots are extremely rare, and if you only take those, you will end up taking very few shots in your life.

QUANTITY OVER QUALITY

Progress in life is determined by the number of shots we take and not the quality of the shots. Your intuition might initially tell you the opposite. Quality over quantity, right? But quality is a by-product of quantity. A tennis player will produce more perfect serves by practicing a thousand of them, not by only serving when she feels she can do it perfectly. Many experiments have been done on this topic. One involved two teams of student photographers. One team was told to take as many photos as possible throughout the semester as they will be graded on the number of photos they take. While the other team was told they would be graded on the quality of their photos, if all they took was one photo, they would get an A as long as it looked perfect. Which team do you think produced higher-quality photos? Ironically, it was the first team. And all because the second team didn't get enough chances to practice their craft. More photographs by the first team led to more opportunities to produce magical pictures and elevate their photography skills.

When we let the desire for perfection prevent us from taking a shot that might not be perfect, we end up confining ourselves to a small number of opportunities. We become an army that fires only a few bullets when we are supposed to be firing a machine gun. Not all the shots from the machine gun will hit the target; in fact, most of them will miss. But we greatly increase our chances that we will hit something when we increase the number of shots. Of course, this doesn't mean that we should take mindless shots that are aimed randomly or haven't been thought through. That's a waste of resources. There's a difference between taking frequent shots at a target that is in range, with a clear strategy in mind, and just opening fire with our eyes closed.

One of the reasons we postpone taking our shot is because, subconsciously, we are either afraid or anxious with regards to what will come next if we take that leap. So, we postpone, with the excuse that we are waiting for the target to be in a better position. In reality, we are perhaps hoping that something will happen that takes the target out of our range of sight. That way, it's out of our hands. We don't have to explain our inaction and we don't have to deal with the consequences of taking it—failure, perhaps, or new and frightening responsibilities.

A common rationale we give for not shooting our shot is *distractions* or *interference*. We feel there may be too many things happening in the background that might collide with our shot. For example, you might think that your children are too young for you to start a a new project or a business and they need too much of your time. We postpone pulling the trigger, waiting for the moment when there are no more distractions. But most of the time, it's our target that disappears, not the distractions. Or perhaps the distractions increase. Your children could grow into teenagers that need more support than they did when they were little. And the business opportunity that was so ripe for exploration may have already been bled dry by others at this point.

Sometimes, we are presented with opportunities in life that suddenly appear out of nowhere. But it's what we do with these opportunities that matters. We must not let our thoughts linger around the imperfections that surround those opportunities and the repositioning we could do to make them more perfect. If we find excuses to avoid taking action and to bide our time, we may find them slipping through our fingers. We will perhaps blame "fate" in these instances, but in reality, it's about our own fears and anxieties; our lack of confidence to take that leap. Instead, we must take a deep breath and capture our destiny with both hands before it flutters away like a frightened songbird, never to return.

TEN

CHOOSE YOUR PERSONALITY

You cannot change your destination overnight, but you can change your direction overnight.

—JIM ROHN

We change our fashion styles, our cars, and our diets, but we rarely change our personality. You might be thinking that the chapter title is some kind of trick statement. I can *choose* my personality? Just like I can change my clothing style? Are you serious? How is this possible?

First, let's discuss what a personality is. When you think of a personality, what comes to mind? A person's qualities perhaps? Caring, friendly, attentive, generous. These are qualities that you might use to describe someone. These qualities usually extend from subconscious beliefs that we have, based on how we view the world and life in general. For instance, if being liked is very important to us, we might subconsciously believe that we need to be nice to people to ensure that happens. Or we might subconsciously believe that the most important thing in life is to serve other people and help them, leading us to be kind and supportive. As you can see, our subconscious beliefs produce our personality.

These examples show us how two different beliefs or set of priorities can produce the same set of traits. In both cases, they produce a personality that is regarded as nice and helpful. If we go to a deeper level, below our beliefs and worldview, we find our identity. This is based on how we view ourselves and what we decide to align with. This provides the foundation for everything else. These layers were formed very early in our childhood. We subconsciously chose our personality when we were kids. Perhaps the best evidence of that is when you see two biological twins with an identical set of genes who grew up in the same household but have completely different personalities. We didn't choose our personality upfront, like ordering a set menu at a restaurant. It formed more like gradual brush strokes on a white canvas. The impact of each stroke on its own is barely noticeable, but when all the brush strokes accumulate, it produces a unique painting.

For example, in our early childhood, we will experience our first encounter with another child our age. You probably can't remember such an encounter yourself, but you may have seen it happening between children in real life or in videos. An encounter usually starts with a very curious look on at least one of the children's faces; you can see in their eyes that their mind is busy calculating their next move. After a few seconds, that child will usually take a physical action; they might choose to hug the other child or possibly even hit them. That was your first subconscious choice of personality. To hug or to hit? The adults looking on would usually interfere at this point. If it's a hug, you might hear them making all kinds of cute sounds in approval of what the child did. If it was an attack instead of a hug, you might hear them rebuking their child, or they might not comment at all. If it's the latter, this might provide the foundation for a violent personality to form. If someone was allowed to be violent from a young age, and they were not checked by their parents for this behavior, they may develop a belief that there's no consequences to their aggression. The reaction of your parents will reinforce or change your first subconscious choice of personality. And it is not just your parents but everyone you interact with at that age. For instance, if you had chosen to hug the other child, but instead of hugging you back they chose to take a few steps back or even push you away, it may likely discourage you from leading with generous physical acts in the future. It might even shape you to become a more shy and reserved person.

Why Is It So Hard to Change?

That is the history of our personality and how it forms. Although we might not remember it, we did choose it ourselves. And because we chose it once, we can choose it again. You don't need to serve a life sentence in the personality that you subconsciously chose as a child. So why is it then that very few of us are able to change our personalities even if we wanted to?

Because of what we tell ourselves. We have strong beliefs on this topic. We have all uttered the following words many times: "*It's just my nature. I can't do anything about it.*" Or, "*I wish I could change!*" We are confident that the personality we live with is something rigid that defines who we are and limits who we can become. We think it's harder to change than our facial features. The older we become, the more this belief becomes entrenched.

As we discussed, this is factually inaccurate. And the road to changing our personality starts with recognizing that it is not something we were born with, it is something we chose a very long time ago. I'm sure you've heard of people that you went to high school with, or knew a long time ago, that are completely different today than what they were like before. We view such cases as mysterious transformations. The exception that proves the rule. They might have faced a near death experience or a messy divorce that convinced them of the need to change. But this ability to undergo and embrace such fundamental change should be the norm. We don't need to wait for the brutal forces of life to give us a traumatic experience, whether physical or mental, in order to grasp this opportunity. We can change when we want to.

A THREE-STEP PLAN TO CHANGE YOUR PERSONALITY

We might sometimes crave change in our character. We may hope for an improved personality and a better lifestyle as a result. As I've said, the biggest barrier to that is our strongly held belief that we can't change our nature since it has been like that for as long as we can remember. Ironically, we are working against ourselves. This is a lie that we are not consciously aware of, but becoming conscious of it is the first realization we need to have in our journey toward building a personality of our choosing.

There is a second realization we need to have; a truth that obstructs our progress. It is what makes us cling to our current personality despite our wish to change: familiarity. Despite some of the reservations we may have about our personality, it is something we are very familiar with. Because we know our personality well, we can comfortably predict how certain interactions will go or how we will behave in certain situations. That gives us a sense of security and reassurance. By changing our personality and becoming someone we have never been before, we are going into unchartered territory. It is sailing into the unknown. We have been swept into the choppy waters of unpredictability. Subsequently, we subconsciously cling to the comfort of familiarity. It is like choosing to continue living with a partner that you have long since stopped loving or being interested in. They might not be the most exciting person in the world, but you know them very well, their good and bad traits. Despite the obvious advantages of moving on and finding someone who excites you and gives you a more thrilling future, these benefits come with an unpredictability that causes us fear. Fear of the unknown.

Instead, because this love of the familiar is so strong, it creates inertia. We subconsciously choose to remain as we are and refuse to change. If we are not conscious of this familiarity trap, we will find ourselves resorting to living in the realm of possibility that we discussed in chapter 2. We will end up saying things to ourselves such as: "If only I had a more patient personality, I would have made a lot less mistakes and would have been more successful." And, "If only I was more balanced, I wouldn't have always found myself shuttling between one extreme and the other."

Some people might wonder, why would I *want* to change my personality? I am very comfortable with who I am and I don't need to make adjustments. Well, it's good to be comfortable with who we are. But being comfortable with who we are and having goals to improve can go together. You might not be aware of how much you can still improve yourself or how much more enjoyable life could be if you made certain changes to your personality. These could be eliminating weak points that define your personality such as having a very short temper, getting stressed about small things, being overly frugal, or being self-centered. We may have historically justified those traits by saying, "Nobody's perfect." Yes, nobody is, but isn't it empowering to realize these traits are things that we can change if we want to?

I used to have a trait that defined my character. I was nicknamed Supersonic because of how fast I moved in whatever I was doing in life. I always felt an instinctive urge to accomplish any goal as quickly as possible. During college, one of my mentors said to me, "You are trying to pack ten years into every year." But that was the pace I was accustomed to moving. It wasn't fast for me; it was what I considered normal. Despite the many career advantages that such a pace brings, it also brought a lot of disadvantages. The more quickly you move, the more likely that you will break things in the process. And I broke my fair share.

After a lifetime of being supersonic, I decided I'd had enough; I did not want to move with lightning speed anymore. I wanted to take my time when deciding what to do and give the process space to breathe. Nothing had to be conquered today—it could take all week, all month, or even all year. It would take as long as it needed to take. I had changed so much, my girlfriend at the time started saying, "I like laid-back Sherife." That became my new nickname. Dr. Reda, my mother's uncle, who lives in the UK, once jokingly commented: "You are so laid-back now, you are practically horizontal." I loved that comment. It was a gigantic transformation. I went from one extreme to another and I had rid myself of a trait that used to be an intrinsic part of who I was. Not only that. It was a trait that defined me; a super power; something I had always regarded as one of my biggest strengths.

From that point on, it was as if I had discovered a different world. I realized that it wasn't that fast is good and slow is bad. They are completely different ways to experience life and they bring about entirely distinctive journeys. There is something to appreciate and enjoy about each one. I was more open from this point on to experiencing life differently and not just in the way I always knew and favored.

I hope this story shows you that there are several good reasons for you to change your personality. Even if it is not obvious why you should, take some time to reflect. It might be eliminating traits that are handicapping you, but it might also be amplifying ones that will benefit you, or even just experiencing life in a different way. There is a big opportunity cost when we live our whole lives in one specific way. Why stick with only one lifestyle and one character when there are so many flavors to experience in life? It is like eating the same dish every day. Even if it's delicious, think of all the diverse cuisine that we are missing out on?

The third and final realization in our journey toward personality change is a powerful one. It's the reason why most people that are determined to change their personality end up failing. You might have tried to be a better listener, a more friendly person, or an early riser. You might have tried to quit some bad habits like smoking or junk food. Or you might have tried to pick up some new good habits like exercise or a new hobby. Most of these attempts end in failure because you are trying to change your traits and habits directly. In order to change these, you must first focus your energy on changing your identity and worldview. This is where they spring from. Change your identity first, and you will find it much easier to change a character trait, a habit, or your lifestyle, as these are merely by-products of that foundation.

Imagine you are trying to quit smoking or vaping. Perhaps the approach you have been taking is to try to reduce the number of times you smoke in a day. Every time you feel the urge to smoke, it becomes an agonizing battle that you eventually lose. You end up reaching out for a cigarette to appease the urge. As the saying goes, "Old habits die hard." They have become so entrenched in you that it's very hard not to give in. This is unless you change something beforehand: you. If you start to see yourself as someone that does not smoke because it's ignorant to voluntarily pour so many toxins into your body, it will be much easier to fight the urge. In fact, you might be surprised to see that you don't even feel the urge anymore. That's because it is easier to stop doing something that does not align with your identity.

A New Perspective on an Old Problem

The Coptic Orthodox Church is one of the most ancient churches in Christianity. It was founded by Saint Mark, an apostle of Jesus and one of the four men who wrote the gospels of the New Testament in the Bible. It began in Alexandria, Egypt, only around ten years after the crucifixion of Christ. In the first five centuries of Christianity, before the Arab invasion of Egypt, the Coptic Church had produced more scholarly knowledge and apologetics in Christian theology and sacrificed more martyrs under persecution than any other church at the time. It was where the first Christian monks came from. It was a church that was deeply Christian when the Roman Empire was still pagan and viciously persecuting Christians. With roots in Jesus's closest circle and the ancient Egyptians, it is rich in heritage and tradition.

I was born into a Coptic family. My mom sent me to Sunday school at an early age to instill Coptic values in me. That included fasting throughout the year, as the Coptic calendar was full of fasts. Depending on which fast it was, you could not eat beef, chicken, fish, or any animal by-products. I loved all these foods, and it was such a struggle for me to keep up with these fasts while growing up. As a result, I eventually decided not to fast for most of them. I tried to fast during the major ones, which worked out to around two or three months a year, but that only covered a fraction of the Coptic fasting calendar.

When I moved to the US for college, I suddenly discovered a lot of vegetarians who cut these foods out for reasons other than their religion. I was curious about what it was like to voluntarily decide not to eat meat when there was no church telling you not to. How would it feel to be out with friends at a restaurant while everyone is having delicious burgers or steaks, but you can't because you simply decided to give meat up, even when there will be no reward from "God" for doing so. I was so intrigued by the discipline it took that I decided to become vegetarian simply for that reason. I ended up being vegetarian for two and a half years. For thirty consecutive months, I did not have a single piece of meat, although I was always surrounded by people eating nonvegetarian food that I considered mouth-wateringly delicious.

My family and friends could not comprehend this transformation. How could someone that struggled to give up meat for a few weeks suddenly give it up for years so easily? They were all convinced that I must have met a vegetarian girlfriend whom I was trying to win over or, worse, that she had forced me to give up meat as a condition of our being together! No other reason made sense to them. When I visited Egypt on vacation, they'd offer me dishes that had minced meat in it and lie about it when I asked them if it contained meat. They were not happy that I'd become vegetarian and did everything they could to get me to stop "this absurdity," apparently for my "best interests." Thankfully, I could still always foil their pranks.

So, what happened? How was I suddenly able to change my eating habits—something that I had struggled to do all my life? The key was in changing my identity. The action of giving up meat was hard to do when I tried to do it directly. But when I associated it with discipline—and I view myself as someone who values discipline very highly and always wants to develop it further—giving up meat became a much easier task. I was never tempted, no matter how delicious the food was, because it didn't align with how I perceived myself. Why I went back to eating meat is a story for another time, but it was certainly not out of weakness or temptation. It was another change in identity that came two and a half years after the first one.

When people struggle to adopt a new trait or habit or to improve their lifestyle, they usually blame it on their competence. They say they just don't have the capacity to take themselves to the next level. It is not a matter of competence; it is a matter of belief. It's one thing for you to think of yourself as a short-tempered person who is trying to be more patient; it is quite another to think of yourself as someone who values patience and will strive to control their nerves because they want to develop and reinforce this identity. It is this change in one's identity, and how one views themselves and their views on the world, that is the most fundamental prerequisite to any personality or lifestyle change. We are not destined to live the rest of our lives with the personality traits and character that was formed in the early days of our childhood by our subconscious mind. We must rewrite our own destiny. If a blacksmith can shape something as rigid as iron, we can shape something as fluid as personality.

ELEVEN

CROSSING THE SUCK CHASM

And those who were dancing were thought to be crazy by those who could not hear the music.

—FRIEDRICH NIETZCHE

B achata is a very fun Latin dance which is usually performed between two people. It started in the Dominican Republic in the twentieth century. It was a coincidence that led me to Bachata. If the gymnastics instructor had not cancelled the group class I was going to on short notice, I would not have found myself going to my first Bachata class instead on that day, at the same studio.

A couple of months after my first class, coincidentally again, I met Jorge Escalona, also known as Korke. He'd created a new style of Bachata fifteen years earlier, which he called Sensual Bachata. Since then, it had been spreading like wildfire around the world. It rose to prominence so quickly because it had a more gentle and sexy style compared to the faster and more mechanical style of traditional Bachata. Some people describe Sensual Bachata as sex on the dance floor. This used to be said about Tango, until Sensual Bachata took over. I wouldn't agree with this description necessarily, because you can dance Sensual Bachata with others without anything intimate going on. But, of course, as with any other dance, you could dance with different intentions if you wanted. But for the vast majority of us Bachateros and Bachateras, it is simply a dance. If you asked me how to describe Sensual Bachata in my own words, I would say it's like drawing a painting with your dance partner's body while letting the music choose the colors. From this point onward, whenever I say Bachata, I will be referring to Sensual Bachata. That's what we call it now since this is the most popular style today. We now refer to the original Bachata style as Dominican Bachata or Traditional Bachata.

Only two months after my first Bachata class, I had gotten hooked. Korke said I was very brave for coming to a Bachata dance festival, given I'd only been dancing for two months. Most people at these festivals had been dancing for many years.

One dance was very memorable for me. I could feel a very strong connection with my partner. She was a very talented and sensational dancer. A lot of advanced dancers like her don't really enjoy dancing with beginners, but she had such a big smile on her face that it made the dance even more enjoyable. By the time the dance was over, I couldn't help but think about how much I wanted to dance with her again.

Two days later, I ran into her at another party. I saw her standing at the edge of the dancefloor. I walked up to her and smiled while extending my hand. She smiled back and took my hand. At the end of the dance, she said, "Oh my God, you have improved so much!" Then she paused for a second as if remembering something and said, "Wait a minute... it has only been two days! How did you improve so quickly?"

There are many reasons why I fell in love with Bachata. I encourage you to look up some videos of the dance and take some classes. I have always loved music, but being able to express your interpretation of the music through this dance is almost a magical experience. The connection you feel with your partner can also be very strong. You can express so much emotion in the dance, it is almost like theatre, except that it's confined to a three-minute song, and you are the star.

Two weeks later, I ran into her at another party. We danced again. She gave me a big compliment, saying how fast I was improving. Finally, one month after our first dance, I ran into her at a rooftop party. This time she walked up to me and asked me to dance. Coincidentally the DJ played one of my favorite Bachata songs. It's by Lola Jane and it's called "Kiss Me." With a soft summer breeze and a clear sky above us, we could see beyond the twinkling stars to Jupiter, bright and shining. After the dance, I asked her, "How was it?" She said, "It was perfect…"

How did I go from absolute beginner to giving an advanced performer a perfect dance experience in one month? The answer doesn't lie in my special abilities but rather in neuroscience.

The Science of Learning

Apparently, it is not how long you have been doing something that determines how good you get at it. It is how many times you do something that determines your level of improvement. That explains why you sometimes meet people who have been doing something for a very long time but are still not very good at it. They simply do not do it frequently enough. For example, if someone has been playing baseball for ten years but they only ever play once a month at best, you might find they never really improve.

Just as we have a system of blood vessels in our body that transport all kinds of nutrients to our vital organs, we also have a system of nerves that allow our brain to communicate with different parts of our body. Through this nervous system, our brain sends signals to our hands and feet telling them to move in certain ways by firing neurons along our neural pathways. As we begin to learn new movements, the brain takes time to register the way we are supposed to move. The more we do the same movements or practice the same techniques, the faster the brain can fire the neurons that carry this specific order to conduct this movement, and the deeper this unique neural pathway is engraved.

If we stop doing this new movement too soon, before the neural pathway is fully developed, we quickly lose our grip on this skill and we almost have to start from scratch whenever we decide to pick it up again. If we do it frequently enough, in a short amount of time, however, it becomes like a permanent road. At that point, we can almost do these moves automatically, with total ease. This has infinite applications. It could be things as diverse as learning to juggle, speaking with a very confident tone and posture, or quickly cutting an onion without looking at the knife.

The science behind learning something new, whether it is a sport, a skill, or a habit, relies on developing these neural pathways, and the secret to developing them is repetition. I improved so quickly because whenever I went to a party, I did not leave before I had danced with twenty women. I even kept count and I wouldn't go home until I reached that number. I knew that was the only way I could get better quickly.

What do most people do when they are first learning Bachata? Most don't go to these Latin parties because everyone there is so much better than them and nobody likes to feel inferior. The ones that are brave enough or naïve enough to go usually have two to three dances until they realize how big the gap is between them and the rest of the dancers. Then they give up and decide to go home or just socialize for the rest of the night without dancing. At that rate, it takes many years to get better because the brain, nervous system, muscles, and biomechanics are not getting enough chances to register and automate the new movements.

Embrace the Embarrassment

Nobody likes to feel like they suck at something, especially when you have people observing you and a fantastic dance partner whose body language might be clearly expressing how they can't wait for the dance to be over. And it's the same in so many other situations. That's why a lot of people don't like being on stage or being put on the spot in public—because of the risk of humiliation in front of an audience. Except that, ironically, the only way to not suck at something is to suck some more. For you to get better at anything new, you first have to cross what I call the "suck chasm." To cross that chasm and not suck anymore, you have to continue showing up and practicing consistently, even when your skills are lacking and it feels humiliating. The more you practice, the closer you get to not sucking anymore.

When you feel that you are not doing something well, I understand how tempting it is to stop or go home to save yourself the embarrassment. But if you quit too quickly, if you do not give yourself enough time to practice, you are going to start all over again the next time you summon the courage to give it a second shot. Instead, the answer is to continue embarrassing yourself for a little longer, getting in a full hour or two of practice. The next time you do it, it will be a little less embarrassing, and so on, until you move closer to the *perfect* end of the spectrum. All you need to focus on is moving one inch closer to perfection. But, rest assured, we will never reach perfection, and that perhaps takes a lot of the pressure off in itself.

Remember that all those people you are surrounded by, that seem so much better than you, were all beginners at one point. They might have been even worse than you at the start. How did they get to where they are now? By not going home and by not missing practice. Put in the time and work now so you can reap the benefits later. Don't stop until you get a little better. Once you start getting better, you won't want to stop.

I had professional Bachata instructors who guessed that I had been dancing for more than a year after they saw me dance, when in reality, I had only been dancing for three months. A few months later, different instructors would guess that I had been dancing for two years when I had only been dancing for six months. And it's not because I'm a natural born dancer. It is primarily because I continued to practice even when I sucked. The more I sucked, the more I practiced.

Sometimes we get intimidated when we find out that other people took a lot less time than us to get better at something. We must never be distracted by other people's journey; everyone has their own timeline. We must stick to our own, and if we want to compare, then we should only compare where we are today relative to where we were in the past.

Most people stop when they suck. The ones that get better are the ones that don't stop. I hope it's clear to you that I'm not just referring to dancing, but rather every activity in life. If we suck at something that matters to us, it doesn't mean that we fundamentally lack something that will allow us to succeed in this activity. It just means that we need consistency, lots of repetition, and a good teacher to acquire this new skill. Whenever we feel that something is a lost cause for us, the only way to rewrite that destiny is to continue sucking at it. The darker the night becomes, the closer it is to dawn. The longer we continue to suck at something, embracing our failures rather than backing away from them, the better we become.

TWELVE

GROW YOURSELF
THE BRAIN OF A GENIUS

Any man could, if he were so inclined, be the sculptor of his own brain.
—Santiago R.y Cajal

We've always been told that the human brain cannot be altered once someone has entered adulthood. The only change it experiences is the gradual death of neurons. These are facts that were established and widely accepted by the scientific community for decades. What that means is, you can grow as much muscle as you want in the gym, but when it comes to your brain, you are basically stuck with whatever you've got by the time you hit your twenties. Your life and your needs may change as you age, but you will have to learn to make do with the same hardware that's in your brain.

Fortunately, neuroscientists have recently showed that these statements are not true. There is now a consensus that new advanced imaging technologies and experiments have shown otherwise. While childhood is still believed to be the phase where brain structures can change or grow most rapidly—this is why children can learn new languages much more easily than adults—such change is still possible well into adulthood. Our brain is capable of evolving throughout our entire lives.

THE MIRACLE OF NEUROPLASTICITY

There is a fancy word that scientists use to describe the brain's continuous ability to grow and adapt. It's called neuroplasticity. Neuroplasticity is basically the brain's ability to rewire itself in response to external stimuli. Let us say, for instance, that you are suddenly experiencing a need to analyze and process a lot of information. That is a new stimulus to the brain. If this level of information is above the capacity you have been used to, you will most likely struggle and give up. However, if you instead choose to continue engaging regularly in this level of rigorous analysis, your brain will undergo a process of increasing its capacity and ability to respond to these demands. Neuroplasticity is at the core of what we discussed in chapters 10 and 11. It allows us to learn new things whether they are hobbies or new character traits.

What a fascinating discovery. In layman's terms, it means we can increase our level of intelligence! People can get smarter if they want to. The problem is, most people are quick to accept their limits when faced with an obstacle outside their comfort zone or beyond their abilities. If someone's not good at math and is suddenly put in a situation where they need to do a lot of calculations, they would be quick to admit that this is their weakness and would find someone else to do the task. In reality, the reason they are not good at math is because they have continued to shy away from mathematical exercises throughout their life. They never approached math questions with the focus and consistency that's required to allow the brain to grow its analytical capacity.

Isn't this incredible? Even though you have always been bad at something, you still have the capability to become good at it if you want to. And this could be anything: sports, playing an instrument, negotiation, dancing, painting, languages, etc. We have traditionally regarded those areas as natural talents when we describe those who are good at them. "She's a natural sportsperson," we might say. Or, "I'm just not good at languages." Well, neuroscience has shown us that we are not bound by these statements. You might struggle more at the beginning of a task than most people because you've avoided practicing this skill for most of your life. However, if you're consistent with your efforts, neuroplasticity promises to pave the necessary roads required in your brain for you to develop whatever new abilities you might want.

We discussed in chapter 11 how the brain fires neurons along neural pathways; its own lightning-fast postal system to communicate with various areas of the body. Think of those neural pathways as trails through a forest. When we are not accustomed to doing a task, whether it is mental, physical, or a combination of both, the neural pathways (or trails) in our brain that are needed to accomplish the task are extremely underdeveloped or possibly nonexistent. They are overgrown with weeds, covered in blowdowns, and lacking any signposts or trail markers. Initially, practicing these tasks will feel very difficult and you won't feel cut out for it. That's because these trails have barely been used before. As we start to conduct this task consistently, however, even if we are not achieving great results, new, clear trails will be built in our brain. Eventually, they will create the physical infrastructure necessary for us to be able to conduct this task well. The more we practice, the easier it will become, until we master our skill completely. You really have unlimited potential here.

But neuroplasticity cuts in the opposite direction as well. If you were to abandon these activities and go for a long period of time without engaging in them, these *trails* will gradually become obstructed again. Weeds will hide the beautifully-made path and trail markers will fall into the dirt. Inevitably, you will experience a proportional decline in your ability to conduct those activities that you've mastered.

This inspiring phenomenon of neuroplasticity explains how the human race has been able to gradually accomplish so many amazing feats, from the scientific breakthroughs that allowed us to land on the moon to the superhuman athletic performances you see at the Olympics today. Our biology simply tells us to set a goal, break it into small steps, and practice it consistently. Do all this and your brain will undergo the necessary adaptations and growth to get you there.

The Link with Mental Health

There is a very strong connection between mental health and neuroplasticity. Large amounts of stress, anxiety, and depression have been shown to damage the quality of our brain by killing neurons. That is one of the reasons why you see athletes and other professionals suddenly experience a noticeable drop in their performance when they are suffering from mental health issues. It's not just that they are depressed and therefore not in the mood to perform; this depression has actually hampered many of the regions of the brain required for these activities and thus reduced its capacity.

The good news is, neuroplasticity can also help us heal from mental health problems, including trauma. Imagine you experience a severe trauma as a result of a shocking event in your life. This might end up greatly hampering your ability to perform daily tasks and enjoy life as you used to. There are a number of frameworks that I discuss extensively in my book, *Super Vision*, which you could apply in order to overcome this trauma or get unstuck. When these frameworks are put into practice, neuroplasticity gets to work in the background. Our brain starts rewiring in order to dismantle the neural connections responsible for unhealthy ways of thinking common after a traumatic event. More than that, it replaces them with newer connections necessary to process the more advanced frameworks we need to perceive and engage with life differently and in a more effective and nourishing way.

The benefits of neuroplasticity also apply to physical trauma such as brain damage from an accident. There are instances where people have had parts of their brain removed in surgery and the functions of that brain part were still retained! How could that happen? As a result of the almost magical process of neuroplasticity, the brain adapted other parts of itself to perform these functions. Amazing! It's also how some people lose one of their senses, like sight, only to experience that their other senses—like hearing—have become extremely sharp.

How to Accelerate Neuroplasticity

There are several ways to accelerate the positive effects of neuroplasticity. Think of these as *fertilizers* for your brain. These include sufficient sleep, eating a clean diet, getting exercise regularly, and intermittent fasting. If you think about it, modern life often means we are lacking in all four. We spend most of our day sitting in an office chair, car seat, or at home on the couch. We don't get enough high-quality sleep as a result of the around-the-clock entertainment that keeps us up and alert on our phones, TVs, and laptops. A lot of the food we eat today is either junk food, highly processed, or high in manufactured sugars and harmful chemicals. As this food isn't very satiating, we graze on snacks throughout the day to keep ourselves feeling full and we're bombarded with more poor-quality and tempting options wherever we go.

All of these conditions hamper our ability to fully access neuro-plasticity, depriving the brain of the crucial *fertilizers* that it needs to perform at an optimal level. If we want to grow a healthier and more capable brain, we should stop treating these as "nice to have" and instead prioritize them. Instead of sleeping whatever hours we have left between when we finish our day and when we must wake up the next morning, we should learn to draw boundaries in our day to make sure we are getting as close to eight hours of sleep as possible for most of the week. Instead of eating what is quick and convenient, we should reshuffle the composition of our meals to focus on fresh vegetables, fruits, and lean meats, if you eat animal products. Unhealthy alternatives should be the exception as opposed to the rule in our diet.

Instead of randomly snacking throughout the day, we should ensure that there is an ample time window where we are not eating to give our body a break from digesting food and allow it to focus on other important processes. This is also known as intermittent fasting. Our body experiences a plethora of benefits as a result of intermittent fasting. These include less inflammation and improved protection from dangerous diseases such as cancer, diabetes, heart disease, and neurodegenerative disorders. Intermittent fasting is very customizable. You can easily reduce your eating window to twelve hours by avoiding eating anything two hours before you go to bed and two hours after you wake (if you've slept for eight hours). This is an easy way to begin that doesn't compromise your lifestyle. Start with a comfortable window and gradually take on a bigger challenge, reducing your eating window to eight hours over time.

On the exercise side, we should take advantage of small wins such as regularly taking the stairs instead of the elevator when we can and getting in the habit of walking instead of using a car when there is a pedestrian route and we have the time. It should be manageable to fit in a twenty- to thirty-minute home exercise every day. You don't need any equipment; you can just use your bodyweight. A simple search online will give you more exercises than you can do in a decade. These are all things that can be easily woven into our daily lifestyle and which will pay huge dividends down the line.

The benefits of these *fertilizers* don't just extend to neuroplasticity but our overall mood as well as our mental and physical health. They once used to be the norm for us—it was just how humans lived—and their disappearance from our lifestyle is one of the big reasons why we suffer today. Now, when you have the choice to make one of those simple lifestyle changes, like taking the stairs instead of the elevator, you have another compelling reason to choose wisely: a healthier brain.

PARALLEL EFFECTS

In addition to the *fertilizers* we discussed, there are other things we can leverage to amplify neuroplasticity in our brain. They have the benefit of creating parallel effects, meaning they don't just achieve the intended results but other benefits too. These include learning to play a musical instrument, learning a new language, creating artwork, and taking dance classes. In addition to the benefit of acquiring a new skill, i.e., being able to speak a new language, the neural pathways that have been connected to enable these activities result in better functioning of the brain overall. This occurs because of increased connectivity between different brain regions and the subsequent formation of new neural networks. It also reduces the risk of multiple brain diseases such as Alzheimer's.

But this goes beyond learning new skills. Travel, for instance, in addition to the obvious benefits it has on our mood, also exposes our brain to new stimuli. When immersed in new environments, our brain creates new pathways, via neuroplasticity, that allow it to be more stimulated and active. Activities that challenge our brain intellectually, such as sudoku, math problems, and crosswords puzzles, achieve the same goal, as do those that challenge our brain physically, such as learning to juggle and doing activities with our nondominant hand (brushing our teeth, writing, etc.) We should try to incorporate some of these into our daily lives because improvements in any of them can spill over into improvements in other capabilities and skills.

A final activity that produces a parallel effect is meditation, a practice that paves the way for neuroplasticity. While meditating, you learn to accept feelings and thoughts that you might have been struggling with and your brain transforms with you to adapt. The way of thinking you develop during meditation eventually becomes your default way of thinking. As a result, you can now access all the benefits that come from meditating, such as a clear mind, calmness, and awareness, in your daily life outside of your meditation activity.

If a new cutting-edge medical procedure was announced that could make you much smarter, with no risk to your health, you can imagine the response. There would be a long waiting list of very rich people. Yet the truth is more extraordinary than fiction. Such a procedure has existed for thousands of years and can be accessed, for free and with no negative side effects, by every one of us. It's time we woke up to the power of neuroplasticity and recognized how we can use it to rewrite our destiny. What will you do with it?

PART III

REDESIGN YOUR RELATIONSHIPS

Two very frightening places
To be trapped is one
To be in a very scary place is another
There is a third place that is worse than both
To be trapped in a very scary place…

We've all spent time there; some of us briefly and some for longer. Some of us only once, and some of us many times. We were desperate to get out of that deep, dark pit. We seemed to be living our worst nightmare. Except we couldn't just wake up from this with a sudden sigh of relief. We were trapped, eternally, in our own mind.

Our miraculous escape only became a possibility when we realized it was a prison of our own making. That we only needed to find the keys to the mental dungeons we had somehow locked ourself in. We only needed to slaughter the dragons that tormented us—those we had created—so we could free ourselves and never return.

THIRTEEN

ALONE BUT NOT LONELY

All of humanity's problems stem from man's inability to sit quietly in a room alone.

—BLAISE PASCAL

If you asked me whether I'm an introvert or an extrovert, I'd find it hard to pick just one. On one hand, I never answer the door if the bell rings suddenly and I'm not expecting anyone. My natural reaction, in that moment, would be quite funny to observe. As I hear the ring, you'd see me freeze, immediately, so as not to make any noise that would let the intruder know that someone is at home. Then I'd start tiptoeing around my own house as I go about my business, all so that the person at the door will assume nobody is home and, hopefully, leave.

Something similar happens when my phone rings. I rarely answer any numbers that are not saved on my phone. Instead of picking up, like most people would, I simply look at my phone as it rings and say, "Sorry life, I'm currently not open to new opportunities."

Moreover, I always have my phone on silent. I find it very disturbing when it rings every few minutes because of some new message, email, or call. Instead, I will check it every now and then and I'll return the calls or messages that I want to. I remember, one morning, I got a call from my dad less than an hour after I woke up. I didn't answer it because I like to take the first hour after I wake up to myself. I want to pay close attention to the first thoughts that occur to me. I want to discover what insights have been released from my subconscious mind after going through my deep sleep and REM cycles. I don't want anything to interfere with my mood early on in the day. I don't even check my phone when I first wake up. I need to prepare mentally for how the day will go. A couple of hours later, I called my dad back. He's very old-fashioned, so he asked, "Why didn't you pick up? Were you sleeping or working out?" I said, "Neither. I wasn't ready to answer your call." My father would never understand such a comment, but it really exemplifies a critical part of my character.

I don't want outside elements to force their way into my life and interrupt what I'm doing; I decide when something is going to come into my life. That includes calls, messages, emails, and people showing up at my door. That is indicative of my introvert side. I am so in touch with my own energy that I feel my peace has been intruded upon if someone unexpectedly shows up physically or digitally. I find solitude to be very soothing, and so I work hard to protect it.

A frequent comment I get in response to this is, "How could you not answer the phone? What if someone was having an emergency and needed you? What if someone was dying?" The answer to that is simple. First, the probability of that is very low. How many times is somebody going to call you in their lifetime because they are dying? Do you want me to pick up immediately, every single day of my life, to avert a risk that, statistically speaking, has an almost zero chance of occurring? I'll tell you what would actually happen if it was a real emergency: they would frantically call me, over and over again, and I'd know it was urgent and pick up. Or they would send a text message after I didn't pick up explaining that it was an emergency and I needed to call them urgently. This argument is just an excuse. People's expectation that you answer or return all their calls immediately is purely down to their desire to freely intrude on your life whenever they want. So, make sure you don't fall for it.

Now, let me introduce you to my extrovert side. When I consciously decide to go out into the jungle and socialize, I love people. There are so many different types of people with so many different backgrounds, stories, personalities, and minds. Meeting and discovering them and their unique traits is like being an explorer. I really enjoy getting to know people who have interesting minds and hobbies. And I love parties, as long as the music is good, the crowd is my type, and the venue is not a sardine can. I love to take my friends party hopping, and we can easily go to four or five in one night. That's my extrovert side.

This is why I couldn't tell you if I was an extrovert or an introvert if you asked me. I am both. It depends on the activity or the part of the day. And apparently, there is a name for that and, if you relate to it, for you. They call us ambiverts.

Although there are two sides to me, if I were to do some time accounting, I definitely prefer to spend most of the day alone—the time that I am creating, reflecting, planning, and resting. That would be followed with just a few hours of socializing, but certainly not every day. I recall one Saturday when I was out with some friends hiking during the day and discovering a new area. As we were approaching sunset, one of my friends asked me, "What are your plans for tonight?" I said, "I have no plans. I'm going to stay home." She said, "Why don't you come with me? I'm going out tonight." She had mistaken my meaning. She thought I was staying at home because I didn't have anything to do. Instead, I had consciously decided to stay at home because I'd already spent the whole day with people and I'd gone out the night before. I needed time to spend some time with myself and recharge my batteries.

WHY DO WE FEEL LONELY?

But there is a big difference between being alone and being lonely. Being alone is just a physical description of our state. There is no other human physically around you when you are alone. Being lonely, however, is a mental and emotional description. You feel a void inside you, as if you are not enough and you need others to fill you up. But there is nothing wrong with being alone. On the contrary, sometimes it's exactly what you must do. You don't rid yourself of loneliness by surrounding yourself with people; the truth is that you can still feel lonely in this state. There is no need for you to feel lonely while alone; it's something you can change. In fact, it's entirely possible to be alone and feel fantastic, to the point where you wouldn't rather be anything else.

To achieve that amazing feeling, you must first understand *why* we feel lonely. Have you thought about that before? What is the reason you feel lonely sometimes? Take a minute to think about it and tell me. What do you think causes this? There is an underlying feeling of rejection that leads to feeling lonely. Beneath the surface, our subconscious mind can process the reality of our being alone in the following way: *I have nothing social to do today. My friends and other people I know must be getting together in different groups and doing fun things. I have not been invited by any of them. I'm not interesting enough for them to involve me. I am not wanted. I have been rejected. I am lonely...* Of course, we are not always conscious of this train of thought, and that's why it's so insidious. Our reaction to that feeling is often to try and break into these social circles that have "rejected" us in order to find a way to join their plans that we have not been invited to. This ultimately makes us feel even more rejected because that rarely works out smoothly. This might also occur when we reflect on the fact that we do not have a life partner to share our life with. Our subconscious mind tells us stories about not being "picked" by anyone. As a result, we feel rejected and lonely. This can be particularly hard on "special" days like our birthday, Valentine's Day, or New Year's Eve, when society tells us that we should be with loved ones.

Obviously, here I'm talking about a chronic feeling of loneliness that persists despite our circumstances. There *are* scenarios that can make us feel lonely for reasons other than rejection. An eighty-year-old man who has lost his wife and lifelong companion will suddenly feel an unbearable sense of loneliness. So does someone that has recently moved to a new city and doesn't know anyone there. In these exceptions, loneliness is perhaps inevitable and understandable, although it can still be resolved in time with the right mindset. In all cases, however, loneliness is experienced as a result of a gap between the expectations we have for our social connection and the actual reality we experience.

To eliminate loneliness, we must rid ourselves of that feeling that we have been rejected It goes back to what we discussed in chapter 4. The judgments that people choose to make about you are their own, not yours.

It says more about them than it says about you. Whether they choose to like you or not is their business. If you chain yourself to the thought of wanting to be liked by everyone, you are signing up for a life of suffering and people pleasing, because you cannot control their thoughts. If your happiness depends on their approval, you will feel awful if they withdraw it. So, the recipe is: stop trying to live up to people's expectations and live up to your own instead. Stop caring about whether people like you or not; care about whether you like yourself instead. Don't depend on the value others attribute to you for your self-worth. Once you have gotten a good grip on that, you will have learned to not feel rejected when people don't invite you out. People can choose not to invite you to an event and you can still be an absolutely amazing person. These are not mutually exclusive facts. Think of someone well known who you admire. It's likely that, if you do a little digging, you'll discover that someone has had something bad to say about them in the media. Despite your high opinion of their accomplishments, they've been rejected, brutally and publicly. Does this rejection mean much to you, given that you put them on a pedestal? Does it tarnish their reputation or make them seem unworthy? Probably not. Doesn't it just sound like an opinion—and probably an incorrect one? If you can apply this thinking to your own feelings of social rejection, that loneliness will disappear.

And why should we be conscious of our feelings of loneliness and how we deal with them? Critically, there are many dangers associated with it when it comes to your health. In addition to putting you at high risk of depression and other mental illnesses, it's a risk factor for heart disease, diabetes, and other diseases. The mind and the body are strongly connected; when the mind suffers, the body follows, and vice versa.

SOLACE IN SOLITUDE

Now that you have the tools to tackle that feeling of loneliness, you can spend more time on your own. But why is it a good idea to spend some significant time alone? There are lots of good reasons. A big one is self-discovery. People that don't like to spend time alone often feel that they'll get bored. But that's because they haven't discovered themselves yet. They have an idea of who they are and sometimes it's not very accurate; it's also usually quite faint. They may not like this uncertain image of themselves and it's often enough to drive them away from finding out more. Instead, we must do the opposite. If we don't like ourselves, we must spend more time on our own so we can correct or validate the ideas that we have about ourselves. After all, you are stuck with you; it's the only person that you will always have at every moment in your life. You might as well get to know this person and find a way to get along with them if you have any interest in living a good life.

So, what does discovering yourself mean? It's spending more time alone to find out what thoughts are going on in your mind. What your dreams, goals, aspirations, and fears are. Are they the same or have they changed since the last time you tried to spend time with yourself? Are these aspirations healthy for you? Do you aspire to have them for the right reasons or are those reasons superficial? Or have they been placed in your mind by the influence of someone else or by society at large? What about your fears? Are they justified? Are they necessary? You can see how many questions there are. You can see how much there is to discover about you. The more you know, the better you will feel about yourself and the more you will be able to master your emotions. If you discover things you don't like about yourself you will now be conscious enough to start changing them. And when you change them, you will like yourself even more.

It gets better. It's during this time that you spend with yourself that you will usually get your best ideas and epiphanies. This is especially true when you combine it with inspiring experiences of nature such as having a walk under a clear sky of stars, on the beach, or amidst the lush green of fields and trees. This is when new dreams are born, ideas for new projects suddenly appear, and even moments from your past finally make sense.

The more comfortable you become spending time with yourself, the more confident you will grow, and the more people will notice you and, ironically, want to spend time around you. We all aspire to be that person at a dinner party who looks so radiant and happy without saying much. When they speak there is such a charm to them that can't be explained. Do you know how this quality takes root? They have spent time alone, watering their brain with nutritious thoughts. They have taken the time to clear all the weeds that were growing in their subconscious brain so they can create room for luscious fruits to grow in their place. That is what healthy people do when they are alone.

Whatever you feel you are missing out on when you are not out and about only exists in your head, believe me. Most people are lonely even when they are surrounded by others at a party or dinner; you can see it in their eyes. It is those who can be comfortably alone that can be truly happy when the time comes to socialize. And they are able to look forward to being along again toward the end of the event. Alone, but never lonely.

There is a story I must tell in this chapter that demonstrates the power of embracing being alone. I was flying home from an overseas trip. I booked a 5 a.m. flight because there was a big party a friend of mine was throwing at a club the night before. My plan was to check out of my hotel late, take my suitcases to the party, dance the night away, then head to the airport around 3 a.m. to catch my flight home. When I got to the party at 11 p.m., there were only a few people there; it seemed like it needed another hour to fill up. So, I decided to do something that no one else had probably done before at this club. I took my laptop out of my suitcase and started editing what coincidentally turned out to be this chapter. I was completely focused on my laptop, racing to finish my work, as I felt the room start to fill up. Although I never lifted my eyes from my laptop screen, I could feel people staring at me. I'm sure they were thinking, *Is this guy really working on his own at a nightclub?* I might have been alone physically, but I certainly didn't look lonely; I was noticeably comfortable in my own company and focused on my goal, unmoved by a need to gain social approval or surround myself with others. Why else would a beautiful woman come to my table to try to start a conversation? I politely explained that I was in the middle of something important and that I would find her when I was done. Don't worry, I did find her when I'd finished editing this chapter and we had plenty of time to dance. A perfect example, I felt, of the power of not feeling lonely while being alone.

To rewrite our destiny and dispel our fear of loneliness, we must not run away from being alone. We must fully embrace these moments and run toward them as opportunities to fill the gaps inside us. Sometimes, the only way to overcome our fear of something is to get very close to it.

FOURTEEN

WOULD YOU KICK YOUR MOTHER OUT OF YOUR HOUSE?

Everything that irritates us about others can lead us to an understanding of ourselves.

—CARL JUNG

One of the nicest houses I've seen belongs to my friend Yves, in Switzerland. The view is like stepping onto another planet. Nestled at the top of a mountain, you can see a panoramic landscape of peaks covered in the soothing color of snow. You can also see multiple shades of blue as the house is surrounded by several lakes. Not to mention the green that completes the canvas, coming from the surrounding forests. You can rarely hear any cars, it's all birdsong. You could spend hours every single day gazing at that view. A calming effect descends on you. Time stops.

Yves spends most of his life traveling. He is a man of refined tastes. He keeps one of the most inspiring art collections I've ever seen outside a museum. He also keeps a rare wine collection and some of the finest single origin teas and coffees to entertain his guests. Given that he travels all the time, you could say that he lives nowhere. But whenever he doesn't have to be somewhere specific, he spends his time at his Swiss house.

There was one exception to that. During the COVID-19 pandemic, traveling became incredibly difficult. Countries unexpectedly closed down their borders or set burdensome travel requirements. The risk of infection on a flight increased. It just wasn't fun to travel any more. So, Yves stayed in his house in Switzerland. He wasn't alone though. His mother, who lived in London, wanted to get away from the madness of being in a big city during COVID. She told him that she was going to come and stay at his house until the COVID situation cleared up. Yves didn't have a choice; it was his mother. When she arrived, however, she wasn't alone. She brought her three huskies and her son Patrick, Yves's younger brother. Patrick never mentioned to Yves that he was coming, and neither did his mother.

Nevertheless, Yves greeted his family and helped them settle into their rooms. He started to catch up with his thirty-year-old brother because they hadn't spoken in a few months. But things didn't go well. Patrick didn't entertain the conversation beyond a curt answer to Yves's, "How are you?" In the coming weeks, Patrick continued to stay at his older brother's house without engaging in any conversation with him. He had set up his new headquarters out of one of his brother's guestrooms and would sometimes disappear for a few days and come back without notice. A few weeks later, Yves woke up to find that his mother had also invited a friend of hers to come and stay. It was now a full house with all three guest rooms occupied without Yves's consent.

As the COVID pandemic seemed to be turning into a long-term situation, Yves struggled to adapt to this new reality. Here is a man who was used to living like a bachelor and who now found his mother and brother living with him with no regard for his privacy or appreciation for his hospitality. What if Yves had plans of inviting friends or anyone else to stay over with him for a while? What if he needed those three guest rooms, or at the very least one of them? Given that he lived alone and was used to the quiet, he was easily distracted by the lightest of sounds. His mother was on the phone all the time and watched TV, making it a struggle for Yves to focus. It became hard for him to get work done.

A few months later, it was clear that this was the new status quo and it was not going to change. At least not on its own. Yves decided to have a conversation with his mother. He told her that he needed the house for one week and that she and Patrick would have to go back to their homes during this time. Unfortunately, she did not take this request lightly. She threw a tantrum and charged him with throwing out his own mother. Yves tried to explain. "I gave up my personal life for three months so that you and my brother could stay here and I have not said a word about that. All I ask for is one week of privacy." But his mother's mood did not change; she turned it into a sob story. That is until she decided she had found a compromise. She asked him instead to rent another house in the area for her for that week, at his expense.

It didn't feel like much of a compromise. Yves could finally make sense of the words that Hermann Hesse once spoke: "Oh, love isn't there to make us happy. I believe it exists to show us how much we can endure." Realizing that there was no hope in reasoning with her, Yves decided to leave the house himself without making it seem like he was upset. He told her to take care of all his delicate items while he was gone and requested that nobody use his bedroom in his absence. He initially considered locking his bedroom and taking the keys with him to ensure his rare possessions would be safe, but he felt it might hurt his family in the process, making them think that he did not trust them. So, he left the master bedroom unlocked.

THE LAST STRAW

A few weeks later, Yves got another persistent request from his mother. She wanted to buy a nicer car and felt that Yves should pay for it. Yves's father was alive, but his father and mother did not get along in recent years. Yves's uncle, his mother's brother, was also alive and wealthy. And yet, it was Yves that provided for all of his mother's financial needs.

Again, Yves tried to reason with her. "The world is going through a global economic recession as a result of the pandemic. Spending money on luxuries such as a new car would be very irresponsible. It's out of the question." She suggested that he finance it instead of paying for it upfront. Yves made the same argument that any unnecessary, long-term financial commitments should be avoided until the economic crisis cleared. His mother was very disappointed. How selfish of him not to spare a little money for his own mother. Yves was surprised by the parallel reality that his mother lived in, but he was adamant about standing his ground.

From that point on, their relationship suffered. Their telephone conversations became less frequent and cold. Yves continued providing for his mother and, by extension, his brother. But he felt as if he had become nothing more than a nice place to stay and a bank account for her. In total, he stayed away from his house for a year to avoid a confrontation with his family. His mother and brother both lived there for that year regardless, for which he never got a thank-you.

Yves thought a year was enough to give everyone enough distance to do some thinking and come back to reality. He decided it was time to go back home. He asked them to meet him at the airport, something he expected after all he had done for them. But they did not come. He had another surprise waiting for him when he finally made it home. His rare wine collection was moved to a different place within the house which ended spoiling most of the wine because it wasn't stored at the right temperature. Some of his valuable art was damaged, his artisan coffee and tea selection were gone, and as anyone who knows their bedroom very well would, he could tell that it was used many times while he was away. Yves was furious.

But he kept his fury inside and confronted his mother with a calm demeanor. He asked her to explain what happened. But instead of admitting fault, owning up to the situation, or apologizing—which was all Yves was looking for—she denied anything was wrong and told him that he was making exaggerated claims. Yves could not contain himself any longer. This had to end. He told his mother that this was the last time that she and his brother could stay at his house and that they should make plans to stay elsewhere as soon as possible. Yves kicked his mother and brother out of his house. He broke the fifth commandment: "Thou shalt honor thy father and thy mother."

The Prison of Other People's Expectations

What did you make of Yves's actions? Did he commit the ultimate cardinal sin? You might be surprised if I told you that we have all been in similar situations. They might not reach the extremes of this example, but we've all felt shackled by someone we love. On the one hand, they can cause us significant agony while showing no signs of understanding. And on the other, they are too close to us to allow us to just push them away and rip up the relationship. We feel stuck, maybe even manipulated.

In such unfortunate situations, there are only unfortunate solutions, similar to what Yves resorted to. Although there's no easy way out, these solutions may provide the only hope for the situation to return to a sense of normalcy. While the shock of being kicked out of her son's house must have been very painful to Yves's mother, it was perhaps the only way she could take a step back and reconsider her relationship with him and everything that happened that led her to this point. She was clearly oblivious to this and needed to be brought back to reality. However, before resorting to the demolition button, we must first make sure that we have exhausted all the other, more delicate measures, like the ones Yves attempted. Only when these prove to be useless should we attempt a full-scale surgical operation on our relationships. This might be painful, but it could be the only way to bring them back to health.

Beware: the first few weeks after the demolition button has been pressed is a critical time. This is often when those in the position of Yves's mother (let's call them "the victim") will guilt-trip the person in Yves's shoes (let's call them "the abused"). Don't be surprised if the one playing the victim suddenly falls ill. Whether their suffering is real or exaggerated, it will certainly be taken advantage of and used to make "the abused" back away from their position. You must not fall for this. The operation must go on.

You must not forget your intentions at this point. It is not to inflict pain or seek revenge. It is to wake the other person up and bring them back to reality. To achieve this, you will certainly need to get other people involved, for it takes a very emotionally mature person to come to these realizations on their own. You must find someone who holds the trust of both parties who can mediate and convey each point of view to the other. If you don't do that, "the victim" will simply tell the story from their narrow point of view to those around them. If they don't know the whole story, these people will take their side and tell them that they did nothing wrong. And the cycle will keep rolling.

While you should stand your ground as Yves did, you must remember that you are not trying to hurt anyone and you must never have such intentions. Remember how Yves gave his mother many chances to compromise before reaching this as a last resort. You should grant people you find yourself in a similar situation with the same courtesy. But when there seems to be no signs of progress, you must summon the courage necessary to make hard decisions, as Yves did. Most people would certainly hesitate at this point because of how it might make them look in front of their family, friends, and community. It is certainly a big taboo to throw your own mother out. But you must not let your fear of judgment by other people prevent you from swallowing the bitter pill necessary for progress. Yves was able to get over that. He knew that his mother was going to feel very disappointed in him. But he also realized that she was responsible for her immature actions that led them to this point and whatever thoughts and emotions she decided to develop after the final confrontation. In this scenario, Yves provides us with a great example of how to break away from the prison of having to live up to other people's expectations. This is especially powerful when we consider the torment that it caused him. It may be easy to say and do these things with people that are not that close to us. It must have been extremely difficult for Yves to do this with his own mother. I can't imagine that I'll ever find myself in a similar situation where my own mother is unconsciously destroying my well-being and putting me in a corner where I have no choice other than to do what Yves did. Because of this, it's a story that is very easy to pass judgment on. But while we may judge, we may be very surprised by what we would have done if we were in Yves's place.

You may be wondering how it worked out in the end between Yves and his mother. As of the time of writing, he tells me that their relationship has returned to a healthy normal, perhaps even better than before. It took a few months after the final incident for them to sit down with her brother as mediator who, unsurprisingly, took Yves's side on all points. Apparently, the source of his mother's behavior was her belief that she sacrificed her life raising Yves and his brother and that she now deserved to enjoy the fruits of her labor (and the fruits of Yves's labor as a successful artist and the perks that came with it).

This is a very common but unhealthy situation, where one party gives generously to another with the expectation that they will receive something in return. You can't consider what you do to be generous if you have an expectation that it will be returned. Also, it's not reasonable to expect that the good you do will be returned to you in the particular shape, form, and time that you want. That's a transaction as opposed to a good deed. When we do good for people, we must not expect anything in return. That's the nature of a good deed; it involves a sacrifice. Also, it was clear that Yves was, in fact, more than happy to return the goodwill that his mother showed him as a parent throughout his childhood as he took care of her finances even when it was not his responsibility. This is in contrast to his father, uncle, and brother who didn't provide their share.

I understand, however, that the relationship between Yves and his brother has not yet been mended. They've had many previous issues, driven by sibling rivalry, that have accumulated over the years. With the right intentions and actions however, there are no issues that can't be resolved with time.

To rewrite our destiny, we sometimes need to take a stand and refuse to conform to norms and expectations that do not enrich us and our relationships. We might have to make decisions which feel unpleasant in the short term and even taboo, but they may be necessary if we are to thrive in the long term.

FIFTEEN

THE DRAGON YOU MUST SLAY

The eye sees only what the mind is prepared to comprehend.
—Thomas Carlyle

Imagine you woke up one day and found yourself under arrest in Saudi Arabia, at risk of facing a six-month sentence in prison. That is what happed to my friend Tommy. What a nightmare. How did it get to this point? Well, I'd like to say that he was wrongly accused, but he wasn't. He was reckless. He got caught at a concert in Saudi Arabia with a marijuana joint in his pocket. The country had recently become far more liberal under its new crown prince and was starting to have an abundance of public concerts and parties for the first time. Tommy works in the entertainment industry and Saudi Arabia became a new hotbed of opportunities for him after its recent cultural boom. But this wasn't Amsterdam; this was still Saudi Arabia and cannabis was still illegal.

My mother and Tommy's mom were childhood best friends; they grew up together. He was like a brother to me. But, despite everything I did for him, he treated me as if I was a bad friend. I'd spent years trying to tell him how he needed to change, but he would only take it personally.

We all experience a disconnect between the reality we live in and our perception of it. But for Tommy, that disconnect was as long as a river.

All that was wrong with how Tommy saw the world around him and how he behaved were put into sharp focus by this situation. How could a rational person decide to go to Saudi Arabia while taking the risk of possessing narcotics in public?

I found out about his Saudi troubles when I got a call from his mother, Cindy. She told me he'd been under arrest for three weeks in a terrible jail where he wasn't being treated well. She needed to get him out as soon as possible. Apparently, he had been caught for possession of cannabis four months earlier and was let out on bail while the legal procedures continued in parallel. Instead of hiring a competent lawyer to help him settle the matter professionally, he just had a Saudi friend with no legal background check in on his case from time to time. He visited Saudi Arabia four times after that. On the fourth time, he was arrested on arrival at the airport for missing a scheduled court hearing. And he was kept under arrest for three weeks until a judge could see him.

Cindy got in touch saying he'd asked her to call me. He'd taken his time, probably because I was his last resort. He must have tried everything else at this point. Other people must have made him promises and didn't deliver. But that was a typical cycle in Tommy's relationship with me. We were friends once; you could even say we were family. But our relationship had degraded gradually into acquaintances. I would only hear from him once every two years or so. Whenever I saw his name appear on my phone, I knew he was in trouble. He would call me after everything else failed, and he would be very resentful about it. This time, he was in so much trouble, he couldn't even call himself. Part of me wasn't even sure if he had asked Cindy to call me like she said or if she'd made this up because she was desperate and out of options.

I thought that every time I helped Tommy, it would improve our relationship. Instead of being grateful, however, he became more bitter. Perhaps because it made him feel helpless when he realized he had no other choice but to come to me despite his strong preference not to. He would act like I'd rubbed his powerlessness in his face. He would never say thank you, never show respect, and never even fully pay back any money he borrowed, even though he could afford to. He would just demand the help he needed without any consideration for his dismal track record with me.

I felt very sorry for his mother Cindy. It was evident from her voice how much she had suffered in the last three weeks. She told me her doctor suspected she'd experienced a stroke given the symptoms she had been suffering. That was typical of Tommy; he was used to putting his mom through highly stressful situations without being conscious of it. Here was a fully grown man, well into his thirties, who still called his mom every time he was in trouble so she could save him. He depended on her to take care of so many essential parts of his day-to-day life. It was as if they had entered into a social contract. He will behave recklessly, she will not rebuke him for it, and he will love her in return. In reality, that contract had another side to it that both of them were oblivious to. He will cause her so much stress that she becomes ill and she will ensure that he never fully grows up and depends on himself.

AN UNHEALTHY SOCIAL CONTRACT

I decided to share this story because it's something we are all familiar with to a certain extent. Many of us have special people in our lives that we do things for out of love without realizing that there is an unhealthy social contract hidden in the background. We are even happy, sometimes, to experience pain for those that we love, verifying our own selflessness in the process. But we do this without realizing that we are actually hurting them and ourselves. While the intricate details of Cindy and Tommy's story might be unique to them, the theme is quite a common one.

So many mothers decide to sacrifice their life and their health for their children, for example. Perhaps they give up their career aspirations to look after them and lose their own agency in the process, feeling resentment later on when their children don't provide for them in the way they want. We saw this in the story of Yves and his mother. Or maybe they continue to care for them as if they were still children long into adulthood, doing their laundry, cooking their dinners, and cleaning their houses. What they might see as selfless "love" in this scenario is actually the opposite as it never gives their adult child the chance to stand on their own two feet and reach their full potential.

In the case of Tommy and Cindy, I like to believe that neither of them were conscious of their social contract. Perhaps Tommy just thought that all mothers worry and wasn't aware of the high level of stress he was causing. Perhaps he showered her with gifts to demonstrate his love. Nevertheless, there was no question that this relationship was extremely damaging to both of them. It also made Tommy bitter when anyone like me tried to rectify his behavior because he'd become conditioned by his mom's behavior to believe that anyone who loves you will not scold you and will let you go on as you are. But when your behavior is leading you toward spending six months in a Saudi prison, I don't see how anyone who loves you could take such an approach.

Throughout my history with Tommy, when all hope was lost of him listening to me, I always tried to convince his mother instead. During the Saudi incident, I tried to explain how damaging their current relationship was. He was highly dependent on her, which was draining her physical and mental health, but she would never admit that. My conversations with her didn't go anywhere. But on my last call with her, I could sense she had had enough of the insufferable pain she was in. But her answer to this was frustratingly specific to the scenario at hand: it was time he stopped recreational drugs, she said. She decided to be very firm with him when he returned for the very first time in their relationship.

Ultimately, I realized that they both shared the same delusional nature. Her perception of the situation was that the biggest problem her son had was recreational drugs! Not the fact that he consciously decided to carry drugs with him in a country like Saudi Arabia that has extreme penalties for drug use and possession. Not the fact that after he got lucky and was released on bail the first time, he failed to resolve the legal situation and entrust it to a professional lawyer. I told her clearly that if her conclusion was that his drug problem was the only issue at stake, she was wasting her own time as well as mine. She was the only person who could do anything about these overarching problems but she was unwilling to see them.

She wanted me to get him out of prison as soon as possible, but I explained that if it was too easy, he would never change. I wouldn't let him serve his prison term if he was sentenced, but as he was guilty of the charges, there was an opportunity for him to learn from the period he would spend in jail while the trial was ongoing. If we helped him get out easily and there were no consequences to his actions, he'd never see the need to alter his behavior. This is a great experience for him, I argued. He will have the chance to spend some time with himself and to rewind the last few months in his head and ask some questions. How did I end up here? Was it something I did? Has this situation played out before in a different form? Is there a pattern that I have been repeating? Are there things that need to change in my thinking and behavior? Have I been confident about how I perceive certain things, while in reality, I was actually completely wrong?

Tommy, however, would have taken my reaction as a form of punishment. He was used to being loved and accepted regardless of what he did wrong and without any effort to prevent the same mistakes from happening again in the future. I never intended to punish him, only to help him learn from his mistakes. But what was in his head was in his head. He wouldn't see it any other way.

Are You Ignoring the Dragon?

Tommy and his mom were both suffering. Every time she talked to me while he was in jail, I felt like she was becoming more unwell from the stress she was inflicting on herself. She could not differentiate between a situation of pure suffering and a painful situation that is meant to teach you something and rectify your course in life. There was a dragon that needed to be slayed. It was the only way that the suffering could end. If she didn't slay the dragon once and for all, it would only return later, again and again.

But what was the dragon in this story? What needed to be slayed? It was the social contract between Tommy and his mom Cindy. Cindy was making the same mistake many of us make. As long as she ignored the dragon's existence, there was no need to face it. It was perhaps more comfortable to ignore the fact she needed to make such a fundamental change in her life, but ironically, the more Cindy ignored the existence of the dragon, the more she suffered. As the dragon made sudden reappearances in her life, each was more significant than the one before and more painful. It is as if, the more his presence was ignored, the larger the dragon was growing in size; his powers were only becoming greater.

Tommy needed to slay the same dragon as well. Yet he too chose to ignore its existence. He had a shocking level of dependance on his mother, but he could never admit that because that would mean admitting a problem existed. He had to find different labels for the relationship. Instead, Tommy chose to bathe in the comfort that his mom provided while postponing the inevitable suffering that would come once his mother was no longer there in this world.

Wherever there is suffering, there is a dragon to be slain. Emotional pain is a signal, not a punishment. When you feel it, it's telling you that there is something wrong in your life. That something needs to be rectified. Usually, when we feel discomfort, our first inclination is to try to make it go away. We search for any means available to numb the pain. We ignore the existence of the dragon. But if we do not muster the bravery to seek out and face our dragon in the deep, dark depths of our mind, we are choosing to live on painkillers. Treating the symptoms rather than the underlying cause.

We also ignore the dragon because facing it usually entails some sort of confrontation in our lives. Most of us would do anything to avoid confrontation. Confrontation might sound like an antagonistic word, but it doesn't have to be like that. It might cause some short-term pain, but it's preferable to the long-term pain of avoidance and denial. We can slay that dragon for good or ignore it, allowing it to make regular reappearances in our life, getting bigger and stronger at every turn.

Sometimes, it can be hard for us to find the dragon. We can see the aftermath of the damage they have inflicted, but it's not as obvious to us where this dragon can be found. We must go searching for it. Those closest to us can sometimes be useful in helping us spot patterns and trends in our life that cause us pain or get us into trouble. We are sometimes too biased to notice them on our own. We must be open to uncomfortable truths, otherwise we may never know where the dragon hides, for it usually hides in the most unexpected places.

One way to find the dragon is to follow the trail it has left behind. The pain we feel represents the marks of the dragon's footsteps. Where there is pain, there is suffering, and where there is suffering, there is a dragon to be slain. Once we feel pain, me must come to the rational conclusion that there are changes that we need to make. We must ready ourselves to slay the dragon wherever it turns out to be. If we can't make that commitment, we are normalizing our suffering.

We must interrogate our pain with probing questions: What is causing me pain? Why is it painful? Is it the act that is painful or the person that is performing the act that makes it painful? Is it the act that is painful or how I am reacting to the act that is creating the pain? Why am I reacting that way? Is there a subconscious void in my life that needs to be filled? Why is there a void in my life? Do I want to fill this void? Is this the only way I can fill the void or are there better ways? Is this the only person to fill this void? Is this the best person to fill the void? Can I fill this void myself? Is it better to fill this void instantly or should it be a more gradual and rational process? What else happened that could have deepened this void? An attachment perhaps? A rejection? An abandonment? A bad choice? A failure?

If you strongly feel that one of the last four reasons caused this void, then it's crucial to reconsider your interpretation of these incidents. Are there other ways to look at the same event without perceiving it as a rejection while still absorbing the lessons learned from it? Sharpening your perception is one of the most critical tools to transforming pain into progress. I wrote my first book, *Super Vision,* to help people make that leap.

Tommy managed to get out of prison on bail again and made it back to his mom. How was their first encounter? Did they manage to remedy the dangerous holes in their relationship? Did Cindy finally develop the courage and the consciousness to slay the dragon? We shall find out in the future.

We all have a dragon in our life, one that we have been ignoring. And our ignorance of it has likely allowed it to grow bigger in size. What represents the dragon in your life? Have you realized that you need to slay it? Or has it been a while since that dragon ambushed you in your life? Is it really gone or is just lurking in the distance, growing in strength so that it can make an inevitable reappearance?

When we grew up, we realized that the dragons we were told about in childhood were mystical creatures that do not exist. But dragons do exist and ignoring the marks that they leave in our life would be nothing short of self-sabotage. When we decide to rewrite our destiny and make a commitment to our enlightenment and well-being, we will muster the courage to face those dragons. And when we find them, we will indeed slay them once and for all, because they never expect us to face them.

SIXTEEN

SUFFER WITHOUT SUFFERING

The wise man accepts his pain, endures it but does not add to it.
—MARCUS AURELIUS

Let's return to Tommy's family from chapter 15. His father, Steve, was a wrestling champion. Steve was an indefatigable man who spent most of his life fighting, not just in the arena, but outside of it as well. In Steve's younger days, he experienced a lot of prejudice from the wrestling federations because of his religion. Prejudice, discrimination, and unfair treatment are all still common today in most athletic federations as a result of corruption, but it's even worse in developing countries. The system that Steve witnessed wasn't a meritocracy; it wasn't the best athletes that were picked on the national team. Rather, it was the ones who pleased the egos of the officials or filled their pockets. Despite his athletic gifts, Steve had to battle discrimination to become champion. According to him, the battles he had to fight outside the arena were far more difficult than his toughest wrestling matches.

This left such a strong mark on Steve's character that it defined him. He saw everything he experienced as a struggle, as a fight that he had to win. After he retired from wrestling, Steve continued to be a regular guest on TV and radio shows. He was also invited to some public ceremonies by the president from time to time. Steve was a commanding man with conservative values. If you said you would call him back, you better follow through unless you wanted to upset him. He believed what he believed and you couldn't change his mind about anything. He was inexorable. I'm sure you can only imagine what a father with Steve's character felt when his wife Cindy called him to tell him that his son was under arrest in Saudi Arabia for possession of drugs.

He took the news very badly. Although his son was well into his thirties and they didn't see each other often, he still felt that he was responsible for him. It was a feeling of helplessness that broke Steve. He couldn't bear the feeling that his hands were tied and he couldn't do anything to protect his son. As Tommy was in a foreign country, Steve could not shield him. That feeling of weakness was something Steve was not used to. He was a man that had bulldozed his way through life.

Coincidentally, Steve was supposed to meet the president at a public ceremony the night he found out about Tommy's situation. The president was the only person Steve knew that could perhaps do something to help his son. But what could he tell the president? That his adult son was acting like a reckless teenager and got caught for drug possession in Saudi Arabia? Could he admit that to anyone, let alone the president? Would the president even help him? At the same time, should he not take any chance available to help his son? Steve spent the night wrestling with himself in the arena of his mind.

When Steve heard that I could do something for Tommy, he called me to find out how I could help him. Had I not had Steve's number saved, I would not have recognized him from his broken voice. And the word broken is an understatement. He wasn't weeping; it was the exhausted and sluggish tone he spoke even simple words with that gave him away. This once dynamic man was entirely diminished by the trauma of his son's situation.

I SUFFER, THEREFORE I AM

Sometimes, like Steve, we glorify suffering. It is a mistake most of us make. Suffering is perhaps a subconscious reminder that you are alive. You are the protagonist of the story, the center of attention, because you are the one suffering. Because of this, we sometimes subconsciously look for a reason to suffer. We interpret events that happen in our lives in ways that can make us suffer.

Some parents don't have anything else in their lives, other than their children, that gives them meaning or a sense of purpose. They end up precariously living their life through them. Such parents mostly experience pain and joy in life through the pain and joy that their children experience. It is why certain parents can be very controlling of their children's futures from a young age. They want their son to study medicine and become a doctor. Subconsciously it's because, as a parent, they would be happy if their son was a doctor. On the surface, however, they say that it's what's best for their son. In reality, it may not the best thing for their son to study medicine for eight years if he absolutely hates it and would prefer to be an artist. I have seen so many parents insist that their children study a field that they have no interest in whatsoever.

It was so saddening to see the extent to which Steve jeopardized his health after he heard of Tommy's news. Steve couldn't see that it was his son's responsibility, not his. It was Tommy that had to live through this experience and accept the consequences of his actions. Steve should not have shared the jail cell with Tommy, even metaphorically. In fact, Steve's one responsibility was not to let it break him. To look after his own health. The anxiety he was feeling on behalf of Tommy may be seen by some as emblematic of his love and sacrifice, but in reality, it was really only a form of self-harm. If Steve was to suffer a stroke, which certainly seemed a possibility, it would have been Steve's doing and not Tommy's. A stroke would also have taken him out of Tommy's life once and for all. Who would be there to help Tommy mature into the man he needed to become after he left jail?

Another possible subconscious reason that probably affected Steve negatively was a feeling that he failed as a father. On first impressions, if your son ended up in jail in Saudi Arabia, it doesn't really make you a candidate for the best father award. But first impressions can be very misleading. Steve should only judge himself as a father by what he did for his son while he was growing up. What kind of support did he provide him with? What kind of opportunities for growth did he work hard to give him access to? What values did he teach him? What personal bond did he build with him? What his son decides to do with that is his son's responsibility, not his. He can't live both their lives. But many parents make this mistake.

Even if Steve felt that he failed as a father, that is the past. There is no point in being sad about it. We are in the present now, and we have a choice. Are we going to continue the mistakes of the past or are we going to choose a different path? In the case of Steve, maybe his mistake was that he gave his son too much freedom. There's no point dwelling on that. The only thing we can do is change our approach in the future. Given Tommy's dependance on his parents, maybe it was time for Steve to consider a change in how he dealt with his son. To alter the incentive structure and freedoms he provided him with.

In difficult situations, it is sometimes easy for us to generalize and call ourselves a failure. But just because a situation ended very badly, doesn't mean you are a failure. Perhaps you made mistakes but you were acting with the best of intentions and with the knowledge you had at the time. This doesn't make you a criminal. At most, you might have made a bad judgment, but you are certainly not a failure. It is important for us to keep this in perspective. To learn to look at the past and digest everything we can learn from it without being overwhelmed by the mistakes we discover that may shatter our self-image. It is our thoughts about these events that will break us and not the events themselves. Instead, the most important thing for us to do is to determine our next course of action. How will we deal with this? What will we do? Is there nothing to be done? Doing nothing can be a course of action in itself. Sometimes, taking a breath and doing nothing for a time is the wisest decision of all because doing anything would only make matters worse.

Usually, there is always something to be done. It may just be that you need to act later on, in the future, and leave things be in the present. In the case of Steve, the most crucial action he could take was not getting his son out of jail but being there to reprimand and reform him when he was out. We must learn to discern the difference between the time for action and the time for inaction. We must conserve our resources for the right moment. Otherwise, the time for action may come only for us to find that we have no fuel left in the tank. Self-destruction should be a crime. Why is it a crime to destroy others but completely legal to destroy yourself? Unfortunately, so many people in the world react this way. Voluntarily committing self-harm as a response to news that a loved one has been harmed.

SUFFERING IS A CHOICE

Why do we choose to make ourselves suffer when we hear that a loved one is suffering? Perhaps we do it out of guilt? We might subconsciously think that if a loved one is suffering and we are emotionally indifferent than we must not love them. If we love them, surely we must suffer with them? The more we suffer with them, the more people see us suffering, and the more they can discern that we love them. The more we hurt ourselves, the more we get sick, the more paralyzed we are by fear and sadness, the more they mean to us. Of course, none of this makes any sense. But we do it intuitively. It is such an unhealthy train of thought and it is a lose-lose situation for us and our loved ones. We suffer and they lose out on our capacity to help them because we have immobilized ourselves.

We must therefore break the taboo and fight off the guilt that leads us into this mental trap. If we cannot do anything for a loved one that is suffering, we must not make matters worse for ourselves or for them. We have to realize that our goal should be to outlast this calamity instead of self-imploding. We must conserve our energy and our spirits so that we can do everything we can for them when the tides change. So that we can preserve our full tank of fuel for them (and for us as well)! Resist the guilt that comes from the thought that you could not protect them. Resist the belief that this was a result of some failure of our own. Resist making matters worse by damaging your own health and spirit.

Suffering is a subconscious choice that we make when we disable our intellectual perspective on events and let our thoughts and emotions drown us in pain. You *can* go through a terrible or unfortunate experience without suffering through it. It is enough that we must go through such an unfortunate experience to start with; we must not make matters worse by also choosing to suffer through it.

In the unfortunate event that a loved one is going through a painful experience, we must ask ourselves: *Can we do something for them?* If the answer is yes, we should pour our heart into it and help them with everything that we can to relieve their suffering. If the answer is no, then we must choose not to suffer with them.

By suffering, we simply choose to make a bad situation worse; to exacerbate the damage. It is one thing to understand what our loved ones are going through with deep empathy, to feel their pain, and to show solidarity. It is quite another to inflict damage on ourselves for no reason. When one's hands are tied, we must remember the one thing we can actually do in order to rewrite our destiny: to refrain from suffering.

SEVENTEEN

THE TIME I HAD $72 MILLION STOLEN FROM ME—PART I, THE GREAT HEIST

A man is great not because he hasn't failed; a man is great because failure hasn't stopped him.

—CONFUCIUS

My professors were surprised by how thick my college thesis was when I printed it. "It's just an undergraduate thesis, Sherife, not a doctorate," they exclaimed as I handed in my last assignment before I could graduate. I wrote my thesis at MIT on creating a solar energy industry in Egypt. I was boiling with passion for this idea. Egypt is a country that has abundant sunshine all year round, yet at the time, solar energy systems were almost nonexistent. The country was still getting almost all of its energy from fossil fuels like natural gas and petroleum. I couldn't wait to change that.

During my freshman year at MIT, a very distinguished Egyptian came to campus to deliver a lecture. His name was Dr. Zhivago and he was thirty-five years older than me. He had obtained his PhD from MIT and returned to Egypt to help the government modernize its infrastructure. He even worked directly with the president's son for decades after he graduated MIT. As Egypt's president had become a frail old man after thirty years in power, his son was basically running the country. Dr. Zhivago was not just a very influential man in Egypt; he was also knighted by the French and Swiss governments. I spoke to him after he finished his lecture and told him about my dreams to turn Egypt into a solar energy giant. He was very impressed and asked me to come see him next time I was in Egypt. He also complimented me on the suit I was wearing, saying, "You are very chic." Since he was someone that took style very seriously, judging by his fancy tie and lavish cuff links, I was flattered by his comment.

My ambitions extended beyond making Egypt run on solar energy. The country was so strategically located geographically that it could export electricity to Europe through submarine cables in the Mediterranean Sea. Indeed, only 10% of Egypt's desert land could generate enough solar energy to power the whole world! Egypt could export electricity to the rest of Africa and the Middle East, but Europe was the prized market. I discussed all these details in my college thesis.

BUILDING MY SOLAR DREAM

I graduated on June 5 and was on a flight from Boston to Cairo on June 7. And that's only because there were no flights on June 6. I couldn't wait to make my dream a reality. Everyone else was confused. Who in their right mind makes it to MIT at the age of seventeen, only to come back to Egypt straight after graduation, they wondered. They felt it was like almost reaching the top of the mountain only to voluntarily jump back to sea level. I didn't see it like that. The reason I left Egypt was so I could return with the skills to put the country back on the map. I never had any second thoughts about what I was going to do after graduation throughout my four years in college. I always knew I was going back to Egypt to start my solar energy company which would transform the energy industry.

Throughout my college years, I kept my bond with Egypt strong. I started an organization that scouted top young leaders in Egypt and helped them to turn their ideas into projects, social ventures, or startups. Over time, it grew to become one of the most competitive entrepreneurship programs in the world, with more than five thousand applications received annually and a 2% admission rate. I led a summer boot camp in Egypt throughout my last three years of college to train this new class of leaders that were admitted into the organization. During my junior year, Dr. Zhivago learned that I hosted the boot camp in the same town where he owned a stunning beach house. He offered me the keys to his villa for the duration of the event. What a very generous gesture, I thought. I said thank you, but I didn't accept his kind offer. He commended me on the great work I was doing and told me that this is what we must do as Egyptians: work hard for our country.

All the temptations in the world couldn't make me reconsider my plans to go back to Egypt after graduation. There was a top American company that only recruited from the most elite universities that would come to our campus periodically. I went to one of these events out of curiosity and for exposure. By my senior year, I had two partners working hard to recruit me, but I wouldn't even accept an interview. They didn't give up, sending MIT alumni to change my mind. I responded by trying to recruit those alumni to the company I was about to start. Those partners couldn't believe it. People would kill to work at their company and here was this young man, about to be fresh out of college, who they were offering the world, but he wouldn't even consider it. They eventually realized I was married to something else. Something that occupied my thoughts daily and which I was fully committed to bringing to life.

I had just returned to Egypt after college. It was summer, and I was enjoying a walk on the beach with my girlfriend at the time. We happened to run into Dr. Zhivago. It was the first time he'd met my girlfriend and they quickly got along. Dr. Zhivago pointed at me and asked her, "He's crazy, isn't he?" She looked at me for a second, then looked at him again and nodded with laughter: "Yes!" I don't know what crazy means today but, back then, they both meant it in a good way. He was probably referring to my ambition and she was probably referring to my adventurous side.

Just before we parted ways, he insisted that I come see him in Cairo to tell him about what I was up to now and if I needed him to help me with anything. I told him I would be honored. The following week, I went to see him at his office, an antiquarian Egyptian palace in Cairo, nestled on an island on the Nile River. He had the palace all to himself. As I waited for him in the large lobby with high ceilings and exquisite arches, a high-ranking general who worked with the first lady of Egypt sat down next to me and started a conversation. Ten minutes later, the general said Dr. Zhivago was ready to see me.

When I walked into his office, Dr. Zhivago was, as usual, standing upright with one hand on his waist and his chest leaning slightly forward, a gold-chained pocket watch clearly visible on his suit vest. I often heard people say that when he walked into a room, you could see his ego walk in front of him. He greeted me with his usual smile and firm handshake. I told him about the solar energy company I had just started in Egypt. As I shared the details, he seemed very interested and said that he would be happy to get involved with my company and help me with anything that I needed. He said that he would leave it for me to decide how he should get involved and that in return for his help he would take the equity stake that worked best for me—it could be as little as 0% of the profits. He just wanted to help. I thanked him again for his usual generosity and told him I'd let him know if I needed a business partner in my venture.

ADAPTING TO A NEW REALITY

The energy industry in Egypt has always been dominated by the government. The government is not just the legislator and regulator but also the most active player in every part of the energy supply chain. It is, by far, the largest energy producer and distributor in the country. A year after I started building my company, the Egyptian revolution erupted in January of 2011. The Egyptian people finally revolted after decades of ill-treatment, corruption, and abuse of power by the government. After the revolution, ministers were sacked or sent to jail and activity in the government was reduced to a snail's pace. Newly-appointed ministers were extremely hesitant to make bold moves and sign large new projects within the private sector lest they were accused of corruption and ended up in jail like their predecessors.

As a result, my solar dreams for Egypt were buried and I had to leave the country to find business elsewhere to keep my company alive. I had to find a new goal that I could feed on. The world was not short of targets for my ambitious nature. And it didn't take long for my solar energy business to thrive again. The company started undertaking projects in Europe and then later expanded to Latin America. It was the beginning of a whole new exotic business adventure, one that I'd never dreamt of before. I always saw myself spending my whole career in Egypt, building my solar dream, and exporting electricity to other countries. I never foresaw that the revolution would happen (nor did anyone else), entirely changing the context and the rules of the game. But now I was exposed to a new risk. Most of my income now came from countries in which I was a foreigner. I didn't have the same clout as my local competitors and there was no way to guarantee that my company would get paid in full for the projects it implemented.

Dr. Zhivago kept in touch regularly by sending me happy New Year emails. I was flattered that he kept me on his holiday mailing list; I could imagine the caliber of people that I must have shared it with. His email would make me think of Egypt and that one day we could do some high impact work there. During one of my trips to Egypt, he invited me to visit him at his home at the Ritz-Carlton hotel. I was almost shaken by the grandiosity of his trophy wall. His French knighthood medal particularly stood out to me; it had this vintage charm and royal elegance to it. We spent the evening with his wife and daughter and the view from his terrace, overlooking the Nile, felt like a postcard of Cairo brought to life.

As the size and innovative nature of my projects grew, my meetings with ministers and heads of states from around the world became more frequent, and the attention I was getting from the international media started to increase. But something was missing, despite all this success. My dreams of building large solar projects in my home country were haunting me. It was still out of my reach because the government didn't yet have the capacity to provide the legal frameworks necessary. Even as I watched my business grow around the world, in countries I never even dreamed of doing business in, my Egyptian dream still haunted me.

A SECOND CHANCE

It seemed as if there was no way forward. Until, one day, four years after I left Egypt, what once seemed incredibly unlikely happened. A new government was formed and renewable energy was at the top of their agenda. They put a tender out for solar mega projects that was intended to make Egypt one of the biggest solar markets in the word. I was ecstatic. My dream since my college days could finally come true. Hundreds of big companies from around the globe rushed to participate given the very attractive financial incentives the Egyptian government were providing. It was one of the highest incentives in the world at the time. Even the biggest businessmen in Egypt, who had no experience in solar energy, rushed to get involved. This was a huge opportunity, a new era of investment and abundance, and they were keen on developing the necessary know-how to be a part of it.

While I worked outside of Egypt, I had maintained the connections I had with senior government officials in the Egyptian energy sector. They thought very highly of me as I'd created the only Egyptian solar energy company that was able to expand globally and penetrate many competitive foreign markets. My MIT background was the icing on the cake for them. Everyone, from the ministers to influential heads of government agencies, called me Dr. AbdelMessih. They just assumed I had a doctorate from MIT; some even assumed I was a professor. The respect they had for me is captured well by a memory I have of a meeting arranged by the minister of energy; a memory I keep in my head like a polaroid picture. He invited all the senior officials at the ministry and all the heads of the government-owned energy companies. He used a big meeting table, with the minister seated at its head. On his left side sat a dozen of his most important energy bureaucrats, and on his right side I sat, alone. They say a picture is worth a thousand words.

The last time I had done business in Egypt was when I was a college grad, fresh out of MIT. A few years later, I was regarded as a pioneer by my industry peers and I was about to compete, head-to-head, with the biggest tycoons in the country for the largest solar tender in Egyptian history. Competition was expected to be fierce given that the government was going to select just a few winners from the hundreds that were expected to apply. My company met all the application criteria given the strong track record we had developed overseas. I wasn't so concerned about the big international solar companies. I had competed against the big boys of the solar industry before and had my significant share of victories. Now I got to battle them with a home turf advantage. I was more concerned about my local competitors who had no solar experience but had very influential government connections. It was their ability to pull strings behind the scenes to get what they wanted that worried me.

I felt very good about my company's chances. But nothing was guaranteed. The thought of losing out on developing the solar energy industry in Egypt almost killed me. I decided I would rather reduce my share of the profits by forming a consortium with another strong partner, to increase our chances of winning, than risk losing the project. I immediately consulted my investors who agreed that getting a partner, while not ideal, was a wise decision given our uncertainty over how the government would select winners. I proceeded to make a shortlist of candidates.

After thinking about the options, my eyes stopped at one name: Dr. Zhivago. Not only was he well-connected with the government, but he also controlled a large private equity fund and I had known him for almost ten years. So, I went to see him, presented the project, and asked him if he would be interested in partnering with me.

"Of course, Sherife," he said, "I have been waiting for this day for a long time. I can also use my fund to finance part of the project." The meeting couldn't have gone better. I wrote him an email after the meeting thanking him for his usual grace and immediately started preparing the bidding documents. We didn't have much time. This was common with government tenders in developing countries. The favorites for the award were usually decided ahead of time and informed early, in secret, to prepare their bid. The official bid would later be released with a short deadline to give them an advantage.

I was not going to let any of that get in the way of my college dream. I didn't just want to be one of the companies that won the tender; I wanted to be on top of the winning list. I spent the following two weeks working late nights with my team, preparing all the requirements in the utmost detail and to the letter of the tender rules. My company did all the work; we just needed Dr. Zhivago as additional insurance. From him, I only required his standard company brochure and a signed letter establishing our intent to form a consortium between our companies, with details to be negotiated later. In normal circumstances, I would have liked to create a complete legal agreement and iron out all the partnership terms before proceeding with a project like this, but there was no time. Besides, the reason I chose Dr. Zhivago was that I felt I could trust him. He wouldn't use this against me to try to get the upper hand in negotiations as he had been trying to support me from the very beginning. The night before the bid submission was due, I was relieved that I had only one simple form left to fill in. Who is the consortium leader? I felt it might be interpreted as disrespectful if Dr. Zhivago were to find out that I put myself above him. So, as a sign of goodwill, I listed him as the consortium leader for the bid that my company had prepared.

A month later, as I was preparing to go out for dinner, I got a call from someone that used to work with me. Michael had left my company to work with an Egyptian tycoon, a man so rich he owned his own island. He wanted to be untouchable, so he had set up his own water and energy supply to the island so nobody could cut off those essential commodities to his house as a bargaining chip. I had not heard from him in a while, but he was ecstatic when he called. "Congratulations!" he said. "On what?" I asked. "The solar project." "What solar project?" I replied. He took a breath and said: "I have the list. You won the Egyptian government tender!"

The Egyptian Dream

I recall experiencing a euphoric state. I might have even forgotten Michael was still on the phone for a few seconds. That young college kid's dream had finally been realized. I beat the Egyptian tycoons and delivered a second blow to the top international solar companies.

The place I was having dinner was a very exclusive restaurant with only eight tables and a bar. It was frequented by the Egyptian elite and that night at the restaurant provided a snapshot of the state of the business scene in Egypt. There were a number of prominent businessmen at the restaurant, including an influential billionaire that I knew, and you could tell they were quite disgruntled because they did not win the tender. I could overhear the buzz of conversations about it on other tables. It was a proud moment for me as I leaned back on my chair with a big smile on my face and picked up the menu to prepare myself for what was going to be a very enjoyable dinner. Apparently, the government had run the tender properly this time, not giving preference to influential locals if they did not have significant value to offer in the solar energy space. Hindsight is a dangerous thing in such situations, but I recall thinking that I would have won the tender alone without a partner as my concerns and motivations for getting one turned out to be unfounded. But, then again, better safe than sorry.

A few weeks later, once Dr. Zhivago had returned from his travels, I went to meet him to discuss the next steps of our project. He abruptly said that he wanted me out of the project. I was dumbfounded. "What?" I said. He repeated himself, which started a back-and-forth debate between us for thirty minutes. In this short time, it was obvious to me that he had completely transformed into another person. It was as if I was meeting an entirely new person for the first time. And that new person was the polar opposite of the one I had known for the last ten years, or at least thought I knew. I told him many things: "You can't do this to me…I did all the work…this is my dream…I'm going to fight for it." He looked at me and responded very calmly. "OK, Sherife. Fight for it."

It was my $72 million project, and Dr. Zhivago decided he was going to steal it from me. I went back to my office and started thinking about how I was going to fight back. I didn't say anything to my colleagues at the company. The first option I had was to go to the government officials at the Ministry of Energy. I had all the evidence that it was my company that prepared the winning bid and they would obviously admit that the experience my company had was a crucial reason why our consortium were awarded the tender. This would prevent Dr. Zhivago from being able to sell the project, which he intended to do, and keep all the profits for himself.

But there were a lot of downsides to this strategy. First, given Dr. Zhivago's influence, it was unlikely that even the minister of energy would want to pick sides in this battle despite any respect that he may have had for me. The minister's knowledge of a civil war in our consortium was more likely to have us replaced by one of the other companies that were waiting in line. I'd already heard many stories about how government officials within the Ministry of Energy were feeling pressure from Egyptian tycoons that were shocked to lose the bid. I would not gain anything from this move. I would only lose significant stature and some credibility at the Ministry of Energy. Besides, Dr. Zhivago would surely try to poison the well to prevent me from getting back on the project.

The second option I had was to go to court. Egyptian court cases, however, are known to drag on for years. I would be getting myself into a long and distressing legal battle as I sat on the bench for the next year or two watching other people develop my dream. At this point, I also found out that Dr. Zhivago had pulled off many heists like this before and knew the ins and outs of the game like the back of his hand. So, the chances of me winning were certainly no higher than 25%, all to waste valuable years of my life in a fight that could easily yield nothing.

I told my friend Karl what Dr. Zhivago had done, because he knew us both. He was not surprised, but he offered to mediate between us. However, even if he did this successfully, and the court ruled that the project should be controlled jointly by myself and Dr. Zhivago, it would never work. We would have to see each other regularly and make joint decisions in order to run the project efficiently, and I could never collaborate with such a man again.

Destiny can sometimes be like a bad romantic partner: it may lead us on, raise our hopes, play a tune that sings to our passions, and then suddenly toss us out. It is in those moments, when we are thrown to the curb by a dangerously sharp plot twist, that we can't fathom what has happened. Perhaps even to the point where we doubt if what is happening is real or if we are just experiencing a wicked nightmare. To rewrite our destiny in those moments, when we feel beaten and betrayed, we must give destiny a plot twist of our own.

EIGHTEEN

THE TIME I HAD $72 MILLION STOLEN FROM ME—PART II, THE COUNTERATTACK

The devil can cite scripture for his purpose.

—WILLIAM SHAKESPEARE

Upon thoughtful consideration, I decided against both options. I decided I would not even fight for it. If, with my hard work and strategic thinking, I was able to win a $72-million project, then I could do it again. If I spent the next two years applying the same talents to another venture, I could make up for this loss while spending my time doing what I enjoyed and preserving my health and mental well-being.

The alternative was to spend the next few years in a toxic environment that might bear no fruit at all. If I committed to the battle, I knew I'd have to give it my all, and it would likely bleed me dry while I missed the many opportunities to succeed in other exciting ventures.

I also knew that Dr. Zhivago was going to make it a dirty fight. He could bribe judges, but I would never do that. I was totally unequipped for this type of battle and it wasn't one that I wanted to take part in.

I knew that if I could keep my anger at bay and my testosterone levels under control, the healthy decision, the wise decision given the context, was not to fight. It was to walk away. And that is what I chose to do.

Sometimes in life, we can easily have our buttons pushed. We can get triggered to lash out, to fight back, even to fight to the death. This urge comes from far beyond our conscious control, and our reaction can be easily justified. Someone insulted us, stole from us, hurt us, or treated us with significant malice. In these circumstances, we feel a call to arms is deserved. Yet we rarely sit down and calculate whether such a reaction is the best one for us. We are too emotionally charged by the desire to hit back and eager to inflict the most damage possible on our opponent. We are occupied by the question of how we can win this fight that they brought to our door. We don't realize that, sometimes, the only way to win a fight of this type is to not fight at all.

If we were to think carefully about how this might play out in the long run, we'd realize that in some fights there can be no winners. All participants in a war are losers. You cannot claim victory in a war that has drained you for years. Let's imagine that you got your opponent to admit that they lost after a vicious, four-year battle which left you drained, physically and emotionally. Did you really win? Was the price you paid worth the victory? Think about all those years you were deprived of peace of mind, joy, and the realization of your full potential. No, you lost. You both lost.

And the battle doesn't just have to be over a business transaction. It could be a bad divorce that turns into a war between husband and wife; a struggle to show who is the stronger person. Such wars usually start inside the marriage as each person tries to establish dominance over the other because neither can accept the idea that they are the lesser of the two. It could be a romantic relationship that turns into messy breakup where both continue to engage in covert attacks on each other after they part ways as a means of revenge. Such battles for dominance can also take place with a colleague at work, with your boss, or even with a neighbor.

But nobody can force a battle on you. Your opponent might try to bait you into a conflict, but you don't have to walk into their trap. Some people are so sadistic and emotionally unhealthy that they derive their sense of purpose from fighting. They tell themselves a narrative that justifies the need to fight. Such battles are their oxygen.

Why do people end up taking the bait? In a situation like this, you might find yourself saying, "So you want a war? OK, I'll give you one!" It's because when we are attacked, we become very self-conscious about the implications. There are taboos around weakness that come along with the notion of being attacked. We might think, "This person has attacked me because they think I'm a pushover. It doesn't feel good to be a pushover and I can't look at myself in the mirror. A weak self-image will kill me. I must fight back at any cost to rid myself of this self-image. I must be able to look in the mirror and see someone strong." It's a tornado of subconscious thoughts, led by the ego, that force us into our opponent's trap. In this way, we end up wasting many valuable months or years of our lives in a war we cannot claim to win even if our opponent has been defeated.

THE FIGHT-OR-FLIGHT RESPONSE

There is another reason we immediately fight back without giving it much thought. It goes back to ancient times and has been embedded in our DNA ever since. When our ancestors were living on the savanna and were frequently attacked by hungry, wild animals, we had to fight back in order to survive and preserve the human race. In the Middle Ages, when roads were unsafe and one had to travel on foot or on horse for long distances, we had no other choice but to fight for our lives when confronted by thieves or pirates that attacked us during our journey. If we peacefully gave up the little money, food, and water we carried, we would probably collapse and die from fatigue before we made it to our destination. So, even if fighting the ruthless pirates meant that we were likely to die, it was actually our best chance of survival. A victory in this fight was a true triumph because we won our lives. We had no other choice but to fight to the death.

But we are not in the Middle Ages anymore, nor do we live in the vast savanna among wild animals. And it's one thing to fight back in a very short-term battle where you have no other choice if you want to survive. It is quite another thing to choose to fight a long-term war that will deplete you for years and holds very little certainty on what rewards may come should you win. In no way am I telling you to avoid all confrontations and run away in fear from any threat. We can't back down from every problem in our lives. But some conflicts could end up lasting for years or even decades and they will divert you from a better life; a life that you had the power to choose.

It's not the decision to fight or walk away that matters most. It's the rationale behind the decision. It's a matter of choosing your battles. If fear is at the core of your decision not to fight, then you need to understand the subconscious reasons behind that fear. What exactly are you afraid of and why? It could be the case that avoiding the fight is doing you harm. You may just need to build your confidence and lean on the support of others in order to understand your fears and find the courage to overcome it. Yet, if you feel there is no value in the battle, don't let your emotions draw you in. Imagine a mouse trying to taunt a lion into a fight by calling the lion names. Nevertheless, the lion simply walks on without even looking at the mouse, because he wouldn't really be a lion if he gave him any attention. The same action—to avoid the fight—can be right or wrong depending on why we took it.

A WEALTH OF LESSONS

One of the key lessons I took from that experience was that looks can be deceiving. Sometimes, when you meet people, you are really meeting their representative—the face they want you to see. That's especially true when you meet someone for the first time, but some are better than others at continuing the act for a long time. Depending on people's objectives, they can appear to be who they want you to see in order to accomplish their objective. It is like playing a role in a film. Likewise, they can appear to be something they are not in order to feel better about themselves. For example, someone might appear to be nice and helpful when they are not naturally like that. They put on an act because it's important for them that people like them.

Thieves don't dress the way they do in cartoons. They don't wear a mask and a black-and-white striped shirt. They construct an appearance that will ensure people never suspect them. And thieves are not just poor, violent people. The biggest thieves have pedigree. They went to the best universities, wear the most expensive suits, and are regularly honored by government officials. They are featured in the media, but as heroes and great men rather than scoundrels.

Thieves usually don't steal because they are setting out to do something "evil." In their eyes, they are actually trying to do good. Good for themselves and for their families. In their eyes, this can justify their actions. In the case of Dr. Zhivago, while he was already very wealthy, he wasn't a billionaire, and he felt inferior and envious of other billionaires. While he controlled a large private equity fund, he had to beg more wealthy businessmen to invest money into his fund. That hurt his ego, and he wanted to make it to the next level. He did this by stealing my project. That was the good he was pursuing in his own eyes—self-growth. To do that, his mind would have to fabricate reasons why stealing someone else's project was reasonable. He may not even have labelled it stealing. That is the nature of thieves and wrongdoers. The worst dictators in history weren't setting out to do evil in their own minds, despite the atrocities they committed. It was all for a certain good in their heads; any evil that was wrought was merely collateral damage. *Oops. Too bad this had to happen for me to achieve my goal,* they might think.

I want to stop one inch short of telling you not to trust anyone. In some ways, deciding not to trust anyone is smart because, otherwise, you leave yourself highly exposed. You can never know for sure how peoples' minds work; it's an unpredictable variable. But I don't want you to become paranoid. There are literally only a handful of people that you *can* trust in your life, and out of the hundreds of people we will meet, we do not have the ability to figure out who they are. But don't do the opposite. Don't be suspicious of everyone you meet. Just find a middle ground and be neutral. That will reduce your exposure to harm as you are ready for anything, but you won't lose the ability to forge close and meaningful relationships.

If you are entering into business with anyone, even if it's an old friend from college, your husband or wife, or your relative, sign an airtight contract as if you are doing it with a stranger. Don't tell yourself that it might be seen as offensive. It's good legal hygiene. Protect your rights before you get into business with anyone. Even if a good friend vouches for someone, do not trust their assurances. They might call them trustworthy, but this simply means they were not presented with an opportunity to breach the trust of your mutual friend. We need to make that judgment ourselves. Think about the legal environment you are operating in and whether it will protect your legal rights if they are infringed. If not, what else could you do to protect your interests in the event of a sudden betrayal by your business partner? Betrayals exist because it's impossible to predict who will betray you; we let people in because we do not suspect they have selfish motives. Before you make a move, think of all the possibilities that may lie ahead, the good and the bad. It might help you choose what is best for you in the long run.

What happens when the things we think are very low probability end up actually happening? We are surprised; caught off guard. So, we must plan for them in advance. Go through life like you are driving a car and you are not sure which direction the driver in front of you is going to turn. Simply prepare for all outcomes so you can avoid a crash and be ready to respond in time if a sudden and unexpected change in direction takes place. Just because they signaled that they will make a right turn, doesn't mean that they will actually follow through with it. You should still plan a course of action in the eventuality of a left turn.

THE UNLIKELY PATH TO WISDOM

Perhaps what amuses me about this story is that I'm grateful that it happened. As much as it may have crushed me at the time, as painful as it was to have the moment I'd waited for so many years stolen from me, and despite the amount of time it took me to fully recover mentally and financially. And why? Because it was so dense with lessons. Very valuable lessons. If it had to happen, I'm happy it happened when I was twenty-five. If I had waited until I was thirty-five or forty-five to learn the same lesson, when my company was larger and the loss would have been greater, the cost would have been much higher. As sour as the taste of betrayal may be to you at the time and however painful a chain reaction it unleashes, try to focus on what you have learned. The pain will go away, but the lessons will always remain. Some people switch it around: they keep hold of the pain and they never reflect on what they've learned or use it to better their lives. The biggest lessons don't really come to us in the classroom or a workshop. They come from your most difficult times. You might be reading some invaluable wisdom in a book, but you will never be able to fully connect with it if you have not experienced some profound events in your own life.

You must have met people before that have very senior positions at a company but seem like they are absolutely clueless. You might have even worked with some of them. These are people that have had their position handed to them by someone else. They haven't earned it. It's not your title that matters, it's who you are and what you can do. Some people have very senior titles but are capable of very little. Your capability is built by the exposure you have in life—the number of difficult events that you go through and your ability to come out of them still standing and having processed the valuable lessons they provided you with if you were open to them. What's more important than having $72 million in the bank is having the capability to make this amount over and over again, not just because you got lucky or you stole someone else's work. Dr. Zhivago will always just be a thief, because that is all he can do well. It's not about getting that $72 million; it's about *how* you got it. Think about the price you will pay in terms of your values, your soul, and the direction of your life if you obtain it in the wrong way. Don't be Dr. Zhivago in this scenario; be me. Let go of your ego, take the high road, and look to the future. Leave the wrongdoers and the incapable behind and make your own luck.

As I was writing this chapter, I realized I hadn't thought about this story for a long time. Now that so many years have passed, if I were to go back to the same point in my life, would I have reacted differently? Would I have fought or still walked away? I'm pleased to say that I'm still happy with my decision. Although this cruel experience broke my spirit at the time, my character has only grown richer since, and my spirit is better able to find peace. We must not let others force our destiny upon us. We must always consciously choose it ourselves. We do not have one destiny that awaits us; we have many to choose from. To find them, we only need to look past the most obvious paths. I haven't spoken to Dr. Zhivago since, but I'm willing to bet that the $72 million he stole from me hasn't given him a fraction of what I gained from my loss.

PARTING THOUGHTS

Destiny is not one color or one shade. There are more destinies out there for us than there are colors in the world, and there are millions of colors that the human eye can distinguish. Don't settle for black or white. Life is an open buffet. Choose the future you want, then reach out and grab it. You have plenty of chances to take that leap, and plenty more to change your mind. Our destiny, ironically, is emblematic of our freedom. It can never be taken away from us unless we allow it. Your destiny is yours. Don't let anyone tell you otherwise.

––––––

Oh, destiny…as the young one looks at you and what has been prepared by thee. As they gaze out into the future, they can smell the pleasant scent that seems to emanate from your body. But as the years go by, and the young one slowly ages, they feel cheated by you. For thy sweet taste was nowhere to be found, and your aromatic smell became faint and fleeting. You left them only with the taste of regret and melancholy.

Do not despair oh young one. Thou might not be as young anymore, but let not destiny command you. Do not be her slave. You must make her your mistress. You must seduce her. For there is nothing that destiny can bring to you without your complicit acceptance.

JOIN THE NEWSLETTER

You may have finished reading this book, but the conversation doesn't have to stop. If you enjoyed it and would like to get similar insights from me on a regular basis, you can join my mailing list. Simply send an email to abdelmessih.sherife@gmail.com with the phrase "Join Newsletter" in the subject line and you will be subscribed.

My best,
Sherife

LEST YOU FORGET

Humans are forgetful by nature. Our brain is constantly trying to rid itself of information that we don't use regularly. Therefore, as much as you might have felt enlightened while reading some of the material in this book, you are most likely going to forget it. If that is not the destiny you wish to partake in, read on. I have created a summary for you of each chapter so you can refresh your mind every now and then of the most important insights in this book. As good as it might make us feel to acquire knowledge, it's no good to us unless it's put in practice. The famous proverb, "Knowledge is power," is ultimately wrong. If knowledge has no impact on your life, it is ultimately useless. If you felt the knowledge you gleaned in this book was too important to forget, I suggest you create a habit of skimming through this summary section every few months. This should help you to embed the most essential lessons in your memory and put you on the road to taking control of your unconscious thoughts and behaviors.

PART I: DISCOVER THE ENEMY WITHIN

1. Subconscious Fabrications
The real reason we act or avoid a commitment is sometimes well hidden from us. We feel we know why we do the things we do, but many times,

these can be excuses. We can be completely unaware of the actual reason that is holding us back or making us dive in. That is usually entrenched in our subconscious mind, hidden from our conscious reality. In many cases, that subconscious mind of ours will direct our life from the shadows if we have not learned its tricks and brought it into alignment with our conscious minds.

Whenever we feel a strong pull toward something or a firm resistance in our mind that is stopping us from embracing something, we must pause and reflect. There might be a lot more going on in our subconscious than is visible on the surface. We must look past the obvious reasons and excuses that our conscious mind is telling us for why we should or should not take action. We now begin our descent into our subconscious mind and ask ourselves uncomfortable questions in order to reveal our true motives. What could we be afraid of? Could it be failure? Might we discover something about ourselves that we may not like? Why are we rushing toward this? Are there bigger, hidden reasons other than the noble ones we think we are motivated by? Is there something we are missing deep inside that we are trying to fill?

The longer we let these questions marinate in our minds, the deeper we allow them to sink into our subconscious thoughts, and the more surprised we may be by the truth that reveals itself. Let us make a habit of regularly sweeping the trenches of our subconscious, especially when we are making important decisions.

2. Living in Wonderland

We often make statements that sound like, "If only I'd played tennis when I was younger, I could have been a champion." Or, "If only I'd had enough money to fund my idea, I would have created a bestselling product." Such statements may seem harmless, but they actually carry a very high opportunity cost. They prevent us from living experiences and pursuing goals that may mean a huge amount to us.

Such thoughts thwart us from pursuing our dreams and interests by constructing a necessary requisite that can never happen, whether that's being younger, being born into a richer family, or being from a more developed country. Given that such requirements are not possible to attain, our dream becomes something that lives exclusively in our mind, in the realm of possibility. And this is where it stays forever.

Our subconscious mind does this in an attempt to protect us from failure. Out of concern that perhaps, in reality, we might not do as well in that activity as we think. It allows us to keep fantasizing about our stellar performance. We are, in effect, preventing what might turn out to be huge disappointment in ourselves if we actually pursued those goals.

But we must learn to make friends with failure. It is an ally, not an enemy. Failure teaches us what doesn't work. It corrects misconceptions in our head and it shows us what areas we are lacking in. Failure is simply a milestone we have to go through in order to reach our goals—we cannot arrive at success directly on a nonstop flight.

Whenever we catch ourselves "living in wonderland" by making statements that sound like "If only I had A, I would have done B," we must stop immediately and consider our real intentions for pursuing B. If they are genuine and compatible with the life we want to live, then we should craft a blueprint to pursue them that takes into consideration our limitations. Otherwise, we should abandon them completely and not allow ourselves to get high on these fantasies. We might simply be enjoying the rush of telling ourselves these lies. The only way to find out is to do it.

3. The Desire to Be Recognized

To increase the speed of our progress in life, we should align and prioritize our genuine needs so that we do not get pulled in opposing directions by powerful desires. We don't have to simplify our lives down to the pursuit of only one goal, but rather we must distil the different goals that matter to us into one ethos or "spirit." As we come across new goals or desires, we should first filter them through the ethos that we have committed to in order to determine whether it will pull our lives off course and away from our chosen destination.

One of the most dominant desires we experience is the desire to be recognized. We feel the need for others to applaud us for the work we have done. This desire sometimes feels necessary to us, especially when the work we are looking to be recognized for is something noble or an accomplishment that we feel should be looked up to. But it presents a danger.

We could easily end up becoming obsessed with what people think of us. This will negatively affect our well-being and can even encourage us to do things for the wrong reasons. Once the desire to be recognized takes over, we may find that we waste money and time on things in order to associate ourselves with success in that field, whether it's demonstrating a certain social status or meeting our physical fitness goals. In this way, it can actually conflict with the original goal we wanted to be recognized for by taking away our focus. We also allow our mood to become a prisoner of other people's opinions as we find ourselves feeling dejected when we don't receive the level of recognition we expected. For this reason, we must always be on guard for when the desire to be recognized creeps up on us.

To cut down on our desire to be recognized, we must first realize the harmful effects it has on us. The moment we notice this desire building up inside of us, we should direct our energy toward spending more time in the activity that we want to be recognized for. This rewires our brain's circuits to encourage us to automatically spend more time following our chosen ethos and doing the activities we care about rather than chasing recognition from others.

4. The Right Not to Like Chocolate

We usually take it personally when people don't like us because we perceive it as a judgment on our worth. As a result, we find ourselves very sensitive to other's opinions of us and we develop an unhealthy desire to make them like us. We must realize that people have the right to determine what they like and what they don't. And people make poor decisions all the time. It doesn't bother us as much when we hear that people don't like the sport that we enjoy watching or the dish that we enjoy eating, but we suddenly crumble if we hear that they don't like *us*. People also like things that are not necessarily good, such as smoking and many unhealthy foods. It doesn't mean that these things are good just because people like them, and it doesn't mean that we are bad because people don't like us. As long as we have an expectation that people will like us and require an explanation when they don't, we will always be unhappy.

To avoid this strong reaction to people not liking us, we must remember that we have the right to determine what we like and so do other people.

We must not interpret the fact that someone doesn't like us as a vote against our inherent value. If someone professes to dislike chocolate, chocolate does not try to win this person back; it's simply their loss. Another reason we are often bothered when people don't like us is that we interpret it as a rejection. This triggers our ego and we feel obliged to prove to them that we are indeed likable and that they were wrong. We must restrain ourselves from doing this; it's a recipe for disaster and more hurt feelings. When someone rejects us, they are rejecting a part of us, not all of us. And it may be a part that means a lot to them but very little to us. We must instead spend time around people who naturally value and appreciate the qualities and traits we have as opposed to trying to fit in with those who do not like us.

In most cases, we will find that it is only a fraction of the people we meet that don't like us. However, if we are experiencing a period in our lives where nobody seems to like us or spend time with us, then there must be an overriding reason why. This is the time to find out what is driving everyone away from us and fix it. This could be bad hygiene on our side or a level of narcissism that makes us inconsiderate of other people's needs.

5. Change the Past

We often feel imprisoned by negative events that took place in the past because they have already happened and, unless we discover a time machine, we will never get a second chance to change them. Such feelings can have a very negative impact on us. However, we need to recognize that we *can* change the past by changing our own perspective. The past is simply a collection of memories, feelings, and ideas that we have attached to certain events. This impression that we have stored is strongly linked to our perception which can be completely different from objective reality. Often, the more we were disturbed by our perception of an event, the further our memories stray from what actually took place.

Once we learn to change these impressions and the associated ideas that we have attached to events in the past, we realize that the past itself changes with it. That it is up to us to shape not only the future but the past as well. We may not be able to immediately develop the mental muscles we need to control our thoughts and perceptions in real time. But with practice, we can at least learn to reflect on the events that took place and uncover the meanings that we have attached to them which are behind our suffering, changing those meanings accordingly. A failure that used to haunt us doesn't bother us anymore when we start seeing it as an education. A betrayal that traumatized us doesn't hurt us anymore when we start seeing it as a wake-up call.

6. Freud vs. Adler

Sigmund Freud and Alfred Adler are two of the biggest names in the world of psychology, but they had very different approaches. Freud believed that the past is the source of all of our traumas and that knowledge of our past is essential to understanding how we will behave today, providing a good methodology to explain our actions. On the other hand, Adler believed that the past should have little to no significance in our lives. He would go so far as to say that the past does not exist.

Most psychologists choose one school of thought when treating their patients; they have to decide whether they will apply Freud's ideas or Adler's. I, on the other hand, believe that it is a mistake to entirely dismiss one of these approaches; we must instead view them as complementary. When we are tormented by what has happened in our past, or when we are experiencing general suffering and we are not sure of its cause, we should explore our past to search for events that might have led us into such distress, as Freud would have advised us to. Once we have located those events, we must now remember that it is not the events themselves that torment us but rather the ideas and meanings that we have attached to them, as Adler believed. Once we change those meanings, we will realize that the negative impact that these past events used to have on us has been greatly diminished. We are not living in denial when we choose to change the meanings that we have attached to them so we can feel better. We must recognize that the first time we attached meaning to those events, we did it in a rushed and emotional manner. Now that time has passed and we have more space to review them rationally, we can attach more accurate meanings to them than before.

PART II: REDESIGN YOUR BRAIN

7. How Our Thoughts Can Change Reality

For thousands of years, very strange things have been used to cure people from illness. These include rubbing animal feces on their bodies, bloodletting, and drinking animal blood. With the advances in science we have today, we know that these things have no intrinsic healing properties. So how was it that sick people used to get better after using them as medicine? The answer lies in what the medical community now calls "the placebo effect." When we believe that we have taken medicine that is supposed to help us recover from our illness, our mind activates certain reactions in our body that accelerate the healing process. Modern day experiments have shown that a third of the people taking placebos have recovered from their illnesses because they thought they were taking real medicine. Placebos are still widely used by the healthcare system today, although now they usually take the form of a sugar pill.

Apparently, our mind is a very powerful organ. It believes what we tell it. The words we speak to ourselves can take us to new heights or bury us below ground. We must therefore be very conscious of the thoughts that circulate in our minds, for we are either pumping poison into our body or a magic potion. The limiting thoughts we allow in might be a big reason why we are not where we want to be in life. We must garden our mind regularly. We may think that our thoughts are a reflection of the type of life we live, but we may be surprised to realize that the life we live is a reflection of the thoughts in our mind. Change your thoughts and your life will change with it.

8. The Pursuit of Superiority

Most of us feel that we are not good enough at one time or another, but we are currently in the midst of a self-doubt pandemic. This has been propagated by social media, which has become ubiquitous, and the constant state of comparison that it encourages. While the feeling of not being good enough may be universal, how we respond to that feeling is certainly not. Most people allow that feeling to develop into an inferiority complex where they constantly have doubts about their abilities. The problem here is that it subconsciously creates justifications for the things we feel inferior about which ultimately prevents us from getting any better. For example, we may be troubled that people around us seem to have more money than we do, for which we create a justification that we were not born into a rich family. We may feel that we don't have a lot of friends, for which we create a justification that our parents sent us to a small high school.

These justifications prevent us from changing our situation by positioning it in a way that it is outside our control. We didn't choose the family we were born into nor the high school that our parents put us in. There is another alternative to this reality. Whenever we feel we are not good enough at something, we can turn that into an inferiority advantage. An advantage that comes from realizing that we are lacking in an area of our life and are willing to get better at it by putting in the time and effort. This then allows us to commit to the pursuit of superiority where, instead of being buried in our doubts and insecurities, we are focused on getting better and turning the narrative around.

9. What I Learned from Killing Vampires

We spend a lot of time thinking about our goals and planning for them. When an opportunity suddenly shows up out of nowhere, that puts our goal within range. But, instead of jumping on it, we can sometimes find ourselves anxious to take that step because we want to make sure that we have perfect aim. Our knee-jerk reaction is sometimes to delay taking our shot to we give ourselves a chance to maneuver into a better position that will increase our chances of hitting the target. However, we often forget that our target is not a stationary one; it is here right now, but it might disappear even after a short period of time. Even if it doesn't vanish entirely, the shot might not be as clear anymore.

Whenever we see a clear shot on target, we should therefore take it immediately. We should not wait for the *perfect* opportunity because those rarely come and if we wait for them, we will take very few shots in our life. Progress and advancement are determined by the frequency we undertake an activity, so if we take very few opportunities because we limit ourselves to the "perfect" ones, we will advance very little. Instead, we should take as many shots as we can to sharpen our aim. That doesn't mean we should take mindless or random shots. We should only take those that, while not perfect, have a clear rational for why they will land.

10. Choose Your Personality

Our personality is not something we are born with. It is also not something that we have to confine ourself to for the rest of our lives. Contrary to popular belief, personality is something that we *can* change. It is something we have subconsciously chosen in our early childhood, and because we chose it once, we can choose it again. The first obstacle to changing our personality is our false belief that changing our personality, especially as we get older, is not possible. The second obstacle is our comfort and familiarity with who we already are and our ability to predict how we will react in certain situations because we know our character. We must not be afraid of the uncertainty that a new personality will bring. If we believe in the new worldview and identity we wish to form, we should allow them to be fully expressed in us.

To change our personality, we first have to understand where it comes from. Our personality is simply an expression of the worldviews that have shaped our identity. So, we need to focus our attention on changing our worldviews as opposed to trying to change our personality directly.

Once we broaden and develop our worldviews and it flows through to our identity, it will be reflected in our personality. For example, if we want to develop a personality that is kinder and more generous, we first have to change our worldview to believe that our purpose in this world is to do good to others. Once we identify with this belief and it begins shapes our identity, a more kind and generous personality will automatically manifest itself.

There is such a vast set of different ways in which we can experience life. It's a pity that most of us experience our whole lives in one single shade, given the plethora of other colors available that would bring us a completely different experience. Experiencing life in one personality is an opportunity lost. We don't have to change our personality because we don't like it. We can also change it in order to experience life in a different way which can be refreshing, enlightening, and enjoyable. For example, someone who is used to rushing through life may find value in experiencing a slower version of life, allowing things to marinate. Someone who is very shy and reserved may find value in getting to know a wider set of people and being open to more exposure. Once the rational and motivation to change something about your personality is there, you can begin this journey using the three-pronged approach to personality change that we discussed.

11. Crossing the Suck Chasm

We sometimes lack the willpower or courage to put ourselves in the spotlight because we are afraid of being judged on our performance, especially if it's something we are not very good at. Unfortunately, the only way to improve at something we are not good at is by doing it a lot. Let me rephrase that: *fortunately,* that is the only way to improve. I say fortunately because it would be a much less exciting and democratic reality if only the elite few, those with very special abilities, could improve at activities they are interested in. It is exhilarating that even the average Joe can greatly improve at any activity if they are willing to continue with it during what I call the "suck chasm." To cross that chasm and not suck anymore, you have to continue showing up and practicing consistently. The more you practice, the closer you get to not sucking.

And it's not up to me; this is neuroscience. When we learn something new, neural pathways are developed in our body to help our brain perform this new activity with more speed and ease. The more we perform the activity, the stronger those neural pathways are. Those you envy with regards to how much better they are at a certain activity had to cross the suck chasm at one point. The difference between them and others that are not so good is that they kept practicing and showing up until they crossed the chasm. With every practice session, they built a little more of their necessary network of neural pathways, one brick at a time. Embrace sucking at something today and tomorrow so that, one day, you won't suck anymore. All the great men and women have been on that same road.

12. Grow Yourself the Brain of a Genius

Scientists have discovered that our brain has the phenomenal capacity to continue developing and upgrading its abilities throughout our entire life. It can respond to various new demands by building the necessary infrastructure to perform them. As long as the stimulus to our brain is consistent, it will respond by rewiring itself in order to develop these new capabilities. This magical process is called neuroplasticity. We can use it to develop new skills and master areas of our life in which we initially branded ourselves as useless. For example, someone that has traditionally shied away from calculations because they regarded themselves as bad at math can get a lot better if they practice consistently. That person was simply bad at math because they stopped attempting to solving these problems too early, never giving their brain the chance to grow new skills.

This approach can be applied to all other skills such as dancing, playing a musical instrument, sports, and speaking foreign languages, etc. This process cuts in the opposite direction as well. The moment we stop practicing regularly, we lose the ability to perform these tasks in a proficient manner.

Neuroplasticity can also help improve our mental health. When we experience high stress or severe depression, there are many frameworks we can apply that activate neuroplasticity and help us recover. I discuss a lot of these frameworks in my first book, *Super Vision.*

To accelerate the effects of neuroplasticity, we should get sufficient sleep, exercise regularly, eat a clean diet, and engage in intermittent fasting. Neuroplasticity that results from activities like meditation, travel, playing a musical instrument, and learning a new language creates parallel effects in our brain. The new neural connections that are built as we learn these new activities result in benefits beyond learning a new task. They encourage our brains to become more connected and active overall.

PART III: REDESIGN YOUR RELATIONSHIPS

13. Alone but Not Lonely

Loneliness is not about being alone. It is not being able to be happy on your own. There are many people who are not alone but are very lonely and others who are alone but very happy. Loneliness can have a very detrimental effect on our mental and physical health, so we must learn to overcome this feeling to protect ourselves. Loneliness and rejection are strongly linked; we usually feel lonely because of a subconscious sense of rejection. When we find ourselves with no exciting plans on the weekend, we can only think of all the other people we know who made fun plans but decided to exclude us. We therefore feel rejected and, as a result, lonely. We must understand that people inviting us to their plans should not be a requisite for our validation as humans. Instead of seeking inclusion and acceptance in the company of others, we must focus on seeking self-acceptance in our own company. For there are many people who put in a lot of effort to achieve validation within their social groups and *still* feel lonely.

We must take time to listen to our thoughts and emotions and learn to be conscious of them. This will help us to explore where our anxieties spring from and understand their overall effect on our life. When we spend time with ourselves, we understand ourselves better, and we learn to love ourselves. This will ultimately enable us to determine our actions in a way that will suit our best interests instead of self-sabotaging as a result of our subconscious software. The more we detest our own company, the more important it is for us to get to know ourselves.

14. Would You Kick Your Mother Out of Your House?

When the people closest to us engage in behavior that is detrimental to our well-being, we must make the effort to express how they are hurting us and why they should stop this immediately. Often, they have no intention to hurt us and are not even aware of the negative impact they are having on us. But, if we have exhausted all communication methods and channels available to us, if we have tried several times and the problem still persists, then we must make the hard decision to create some distance to keep ourselves out of harm's way.

This distance also serves a second purpose. It makes them aware of the negative acts they are not conscious of perpetrating. When people are in denial, a sharp, sudden response to their actions can sometimes be the only solution. It will wake them up and encourage them to start pondering what could have been behind their behavior. This isn't about revenge; rather, it's a form of necessary yet painful surgery that must be performed for the good of the patient and those around them. Yet, as in surgery, our actions must be precise and calculated. We must also ensure that there is a suitable middleman to convey the perspectives that have eluded our loved one. Languishing in denial, the chances that they will arrive at the right conclusions on their own are close to zero. We are poorly positioned to play this role as we are regarded as the enemy in this scenario. We must find someone else to play this role who is as astute as they are liked by both parties.

15. The Dragon You Must Slay

We sometimes put off uncomfortable actions because we feel they will lead to confrontations that may produce unpredictable outcomes.

Despite the necessity of these actions, we usually give in to that feeling inside of us to kick the can down the road. This can go on for many years and it creates two major problems. The first is the accumulation of the baggage that needs to be resolved as a result of years passing by without addressing it. This makes the problem much harder to solve. It's like a dragon that we ignore, allowing it to grow in size, rather than slaying it the minute we find it. Secondly, even if we somehow manage to finally muster the courage to take action and confront the people we need to, the length of time it's taken us could create a lot of confusion and reduce the effectiveness of our actions. That's because, over the years, we have set a clear precedent that we are not bothered by their actions as we have chosen to ignore them.

We don't only experience this problem with our opponents; we most often experience it with those closest to us whether it's family, lovers, or neighbors. When those closest to us ask us to do something for them, we usually respond immediately. But what if we are creating a relationship of dependance that is actually detrimental? What if the long-term damage far exceeds the short-term benefits? What if our drive to fulfill our sense of selflessness is leading us to hurt ourselves and those closest to us in the long run?

Such dragons exist in our lives in different forms. Whenever we feel we are suffering, there is likely at least one dragon that exists in our life which we have been ignoring, and it needs to be slain. Pain is not a punishment. Pain is a biological signal that tells us we need to correct something in our life. We often choose comfort by ignoring the existence of the dragon, because as long as we deny its existence, we don't have to confront it nor do we have to deal with the uncertainty of what happens if we do. Usually, when we feel pain, our first inclination is to try to make it go away by any means; to numb the pain, while ignoring the existence of the dragon. But the only way to make the pain go away for good is to slay the dragon. There are additional frameworks at the end of the chapter that discuss how we can detect the presence of a dragon in our life and how to slay it for good.

16. Suffer without Suffering

When someone dear to us is in torment, it is easy to find ourselves automatically suffering with them. Such a reaction doesn't only have a detrimental effect on our well-being; it also reduces our capacity to help them. We must realize that nobody benefits from our subconscious decision to suffer alongside those we love and, as a result, diminish our mental prowess. If they could benefit from our sacrifice, perhaps a case could be made for our choice to suffer. But we must realize that suffering along with them hurts them more because they likely need every single ounce of mental and physical energy channeled into supporting them, planning for them, or taking action on their behalf, now or in the future. Even in the extreme case where the person that has been suffering is no longer with us, we must channel our energy toward making them proud as opposed to using it for self-destruction.

We must resist the temptation to glorify suffering. We must break the taboo and discard our guilt—that which makes us feel that we must suffer because someone we love is suffering. When there's nothing to be done, we must realize that is sometimes the wisest choice of action, because the alternative will drain us of our life force. We must learn to gauge the difference between the time for action and the time for inaction. And we must conserve our energy and resources until the time for action comes. Otherwise, we may have no fuel left in the tank when we are truly needed.

The same applies to difficult situations that we experience directly. We must realize that our suffering is optional in these circumstances. It is enough that this experience is unpleasant; we must not make it worse by dwelling on our negative thoughts and emotions, voluntarily pumping them through our bodies. If an unpleasant situation is unpreventable, then we must do our best to withstand the pain without suffering.

17. The Time I Had $72 Million Stolen from Me— Part I, the Great Heist

In real life, thieves do not wear black-and-white striped shirts and tiptoe around. And the biggest thieves aren't those who are scraping a living. Usually, they've received a top-notch education, they drive expensive cars, they live in palatial homes, and they've received many honors and decorations from governments and respected organizations around the world. The biggest thieves are very skilled at getting you to trust them. They will try to do you favors upfront to give you the impression that it is you that can benefit from them and not the other way around. Given how well thieves have camouflaged themselves within society, it is very difficult to tell straight away who can be trusted.

It is therefore absolutely essential that we don't fall for the goodwill that people present us with, even if it happens over many years. It is not sufficient information to determine whether they are genuine or whether it's a thief at work trying to lower our defenses. Thieves may come highly recommended from people that we trust, and not because they intend to hurt us by sending us a Trojan horse. The thief may just not have had a good opportunity to steal from them. The same thief might see an opening with us that is worthwhile, so we must always do our own due diligence.

Whenever we get into business with someone, whether we think we know them well or someone we know well has vouched for them, we must take all legal precautions to protect ourselves. Even if they are father figure, a relative, a close friend, or a lover. If the stakes are high, and there is significant financial value in the project, we must take the time to prepare the necessary paperwork. If we have made the mistake of getting into business with a thief and they find us exposed with no paperwork to protect us, they will take advantage of us.

18. The Time I Had $72 Million Stolen from Me— Part II, the CounterAttack

When someone tries to bait us into a fight, we usually experience some primal urges within us telling us to fight back. We rarely sit down and calculate whether this fight could drag into a war, how long the war could last, and what losses it could inflict on us. Once someone has hurt us, our immediate reaction is often revenge. Our ancient genes play a role here because our ancestors had to fight for their lives against wild animals; if we were designed to be too forgiving early on, the human race may have been wiped out. Another reason we fight are the many taboos around backing down that label us as scared or "not man enough" if we walk away from a fight.

But, despite how ferocious you may be in a fight, walking away can sometimes be the wisest decision to take. The reason you decide to fight or walk away is more important than the action you take itself. If you walk away from a fight purely because you are scared, that is probably not the right decision. But if you walk away because there is no pathway to winning for you or your opponent, then walking away is true wisdom and fighting is madness with nothing to gain and everything to lose. World War I presents us with an excellent example here. Although we were told that the Allies won the war, I don't think anyone can say that we won after experiencing that scale of damage and destruction.

When you meet someone for the first time, you don't actually meet *them*; you meet their representative. People usually pretend to be things that they are not. They are actors in a role. Be mindful of that. It is only certain experiences that will reveal who people truly are, so don't think that you know someone well just because you have known them for a long time.

Thieves usually don't steal because they are setting out to do evil. They are usually pursuing things that they deem as "good" which justifies their actions in their own mind. For instance, they may feel they are stealing to give their family a better life. So, don't expect a thief to listen to their conscience and change their ways; according to them, they aren't doing anything wrong in the first place.

I want you to be extremely cautious with who you trust; you shouldn't fully trust anyone. It doesn't mean you should be suspicious of everyone you meet, just don't put all your trust in them. Be neutral. If you experience a tragic event such as loss, a betrayal, or a theft, focus on the lessons learned. The pain will eventually go away, but the lessons will always stay with you.

ACKNOWLEDGMENTS

I initially struggled to find the people I should thank for the completion of this work. But my conscience does not trouble me in this. After a few days, I could see a face lingering in the dark. The person I feel the strongest need to acknowledge for the completion of this work is me. We often shy away from saying such things in public because we are afraid to be regarded as selfish, arrogant, or even narcissistic. I cannot judge myself; only others can do that. All I know is that, if it wasn't for me writing every single day, if it wasn't for me reading and editing each chapter again and again, this book would not have been in your hands.

Whenever I was frustrated by the delays and setbacks in the publishing process, instead of getting angry, instead of letting it obstruct my energy, I simply sat down and wrote some more. In fact, this whole book was written as a protest to how long it was taking to publish my first book, *Super Vision*. Instead of reacting negatively, I decided to sit down and write. To respond to destruction by creating; fending off negativity with positivity; fighting fire with life-giving water. I need to acknowledge myself because had I not decided to sit down and write a piece of this book every time I hit a brick wall, this book would have never come to life. There were a hundred other more likely options for me to choose in response to the setbacks and inconveniences I experienced. I need to acknowledge myself for choosing emotional maturity and discipline. A decision that will continue to pay off for decades to come.

As is customary, and as I did in my previous book and will do in all future books, I also want to thank all the giants that came before me in all the fields of knowledge that have inspired me in one way or another. Whether it was a question they asked that I pondered or a phrase they coined that ignited an avalanche of thoughts in my head, their groundwork led to my decision to write about these fascinating topics, many of which appear throughout several chapters in this book. I hope my writing and thoughts will inspire your own avalanche of thoughts and actions. I would especially like to thank Alfred Adler, who is rarely given the recognition he deserves, and whose essential work is often copied.

I would like to thank every single person that has bought a copy (or more) of my first book. And thank you also for buying this book that you are reading, my second. Thank you for giving me the most valuable thing anyone can give: your time. While we may never meet in person, we will always have the special relationship that exists between a writer and a reader. Sometimes it may feel to you like we are having an actual conversation, and that is one of the most magical things about writing. I am delighted to share this experience with you and hope to continue our conversations in the very near future.

I want to thank Fr. Daoud Lamei for his love, patience, and for being a living image of Christ on our planet. I would also like to thank my friend and social media star Dr. Yasser for helping me navigate the Gen Z universe and also for having a heart of gold. My friend Nahla, also for having a heart of gold, despite being mean sometimes. Stu Schmill, for writing the first testimonial I ever received for a book and for always being generous with his time. Jorge Escalona and his dance partner, Judith Cordero, for creating Sensual Bachata. My family, for being a special human phenomenon even when familial relations are not at their best. I also want to thank my publishing team, who helped me turn a manuscript on my laptop into a physical book in my library, not once, but twice. Particularly Sarah, Matt, and Ramesh for their patience and hard work. I look forward to our hat trick together: my third book.

Made in the USA
Las Vegas, NV
20 November 2024

12085845R00121